The Desperate Politics of Postmodernism

REHEARSALS

The Eclipse of Individualism (1955)
The Decline of American Pluralism (1961)
In Search of Authority (1964)
Sources in Twentieth-Century Political Thought (1964)
The Promise of Politics (1966)
Open Systems: Arenas for Political Action (1969)
Frontiers of Democratic Theory (1970)
The Political Order (1970)
Approaches to the Study of Political Science (with Michael Haas, 1970)
Saving Appearances: The Reestablishment of Political Science (1972)
Beyond Liberalism, Where Relations Grow (1977)

PARTICIPANTS

Students at the University of California (Berkeley), Harvard University, Bennington College, University of Georgia, University of California (Santa Cruz), Columbia University, Hebrew University of Jerusalem, Queens College, Oregon State University, University of British Columbia, University of Hawaii.

Also Bob Agger, Eloise Buker, Kenneth Burke, Bob Cahill, Angela Cantrell, Arthur Goodfriend, Ron Hirschbein, Hazel Kramer, Paul Kress, Dick Martin, Mike Shapiro.

And others too close or too distant to name.

The Desperate Politics of

POSTMODERNISM

Henry S. Kariel

The University of Massachusetts Press

Amherst

1989

Printed in the United States of America
LC 88-14150
ISBN 0-87023-654-7 (cloth); 655-5 (pbk.)
Designed by Barbara Werden
Set in Linotron Sabon at Keystone Typesetting, Inc.
Printed by Thomson-Shore and bound by John Dekker & Sons

Library of Congress Cataloging-in-Publication Data

Kariel, Henry S.
The desperate politics of postmodernism / Henry S. Kariel.
p. cm.
Includes index.
ISBN 0–87023–654–7 (alk. paper) : ISBN 0–87023–655–5
(pbk. : alk. paper)
1. Arts, Modern—20th century. 2. Postmodernism. 3. Arts and society. I. Title.
NX456.5.P66K37 1989
700'.1'03—dc19 88–14150
CIP

British Library Cataloguing in Publication data are available.

Like its unrealizable
final version, this draft
is dedicated to Asa.

"In art, politics, school, church,
business, love or marriage—in a piece of
work or in a career, strongly spent is
synonymous with kept."

Robert Frost

CONTENTS

Artists maneuvering in a postmodernist manner, actors treating all the world as stage, espionage agents prevailing in no-man's-land, and children playing with reality are at one in enacting their lives in the darkest of times. Unheroic, amoral, and composed, they are our last best hope.

PREFACE

GRATEFUL for shelters ranging from preschools to maximum intensity care units, comforted by the products of industry, we nonetheless feel uneasy within the all-absorbing culture of modernity. Yet we are so thoroughly implicated in it that we trust no alternative culture to quiet our malaise. Even as we organize so as to bring the forces that trouble us under control, we sense that our very resistance is neutralized by the prevailing technique-centered momentum.

For postmodernists, it is simply too late to oppose the momentum of industrial society. They merely resolve to stay alert and cool in its midst. Consciously complying and yet far from docile, they chronicle, amplify, augment it. They judge it as little as it judges itself. Determined to assail nothing, they are passionately impassive.

Their strategy is inexplicable, I think, unless seen in the light of a narrative which holds, as mine does, that the industrial world is indeed out of control, that we are inexorably moving toward meaninglessness and oblivion, and that we can't get our bearings by looking to God or Nature for guidance. The practices of postmodernism, as I interpret and reinforce them, are designed to come to terms with the present and all that remains implicit in it even as they speed up the momentum inherent in modernity. The precarious balancing acts of postmodernists—their politics—have led me to gyrate in ever widening circles so as to relate the aesthetics of modernism and postmodernism, the play of children and the sensibility of holocaust survivors—all driven by technology's incomprehensible, sublime Otherness. Ultimately I have found myself in the company of pragmatists and hermeneuticists, especially those who buoyantly acknowledge the hopelessness of their ventures, who've given up expecting another renaissance, a phoenix to rise out of the ashes.

Like their projects, mine sails under false colors, ingratiating itself by relying on the conventions of paragraphing, punctuation, and footnotes, relying on a comforting movement from subject to predicate. Behind this facade, I seek to exploit the possibilities offered by what Walter Benjamin called the age of mechanical reproduction. Risking disappearance, I have forced others to contribute to my discourse by unashamedly quoting them at length, by using ingenious software ("Verbatim") and an aptly named Leading Edge computer to retrieve quotations from 11,694 books—that is, precisely twice as many as the capsules of Valium consumed in Honolulu every four days.

Endlessly enlarging on the familiar, committed to the morality of an amoral inclusiveness, digging as deeply into the present as I can manage, I am trying to break prevailing connections and design new ones. This is made easier for me in that I don't feel constrained to contribute to the theory and increasingly arid literature of deconstructionism. Implicated in the politics of postmodernism, I am merely seeking to bring what I take to be postmodernist practices into a still unacknowledged context—an orientation that mandates a lightness of being in the face of modernity, of oppressive events that make it hard to relate things, to bring experience into relationship.

GENERALLY WE DO things either because we simply can't do otherwise or because we strive to attain some objective. Occasionally, however, we do act without concern for consequences—and feel unexpectedly exhilarated. In effect, we are then engaged in playful action which, as I should like to make clear, allows us to cope with the life-threatening structures inherent in contemporary technological societies.

Such coping is manifest in action that blocks efforts to bring things to conclusion. Yet because it leaves the ends of life open and indeterminate, because it aims at nothing higher than mediating among conflicting interests, we keep rejecting it in favor of enterprises designed to produce results. Impelled to attain objectives, we engage in instrumental action. There would seem to be no end to our preoccupation with techniques, and hence no way to enter some territory in which we might find ourselves at play. The results of our frustration are familiar: even when comfortably embedded in our welfare systems, we feel resentful, alienated, bored, depressed. Our major productive, educational, medical, professional, and recreational institutions keep disappointing us in some unidentifiable, fundamental way. Satisfaction inheres less in our work of producing and consuming, medicating and healing, teaching and learning, writing and reading than in subsequent payoffs. The point of work, it seems, is only to be done with it—to have it end.

To free ourselves from this overpowering instrumentalism, we would have to shorten the distance between our ongoing activities and our objectives. We would have to embrace a politics which would enable us to find pleasure in noninstrumental activities, that is, in the very process of acting. This pleasure is found, of course, in forms of play. At play, we strive for no extrinsic objectives. Not seeking to be anywhere else, we act without ulterior motives. Play suffices: it's intrinsically satisfying.

In 1823 Thomas Jefferson could write John Quincy Adams that the spirit of playfulness was the very essence of public life, that the pleasure of the game of politics did not lie in aiming at a higher end but rather in participating in its endless give-and-take.[1] To enter politics is not to assure the triumph of justice or the defeat of injustice but to experience its inherent satisfaction—"public happiness" Jefferson called it. Today, it is hard to think of politics as play in its most comprehensive form. There is a reluctance to enter it. Treating it as a spectator sport, we watch its replays on TV. Those active at its center may relish their experience—they rarely quit voluntarily—but see themselves as having sacrificed far worthier private goods—family, leisure, income. Its featured actors won't perform for the sake of performing. Not perceiving that giving is also taking, that, to quote Robert Frost again, "strongly spent is synonymous with kept,"

---

[1] Letter to Adams, April 11, 1823, in L. J. Capon, ed., *The Adams-Jefferson Letters* (Chapel Hill: University of North Carolina Press, 1959), p. 594.

they keep making utilitarian zero-sum calculations. They scarcely consider the arena of politics as that open-ended playground which George Kateb, a political philosopher, has identified as the "unstructured immensity in which people idle, observe, ruminate, imagine, move about, encounter, travel down the open road; in which, in short, they experience."[2] They scarcely know that distinctive space in which it is possible to transcend our obsessive instrumentalism and, yes, compose ourselves.

Because playing detaches us from the prevailing instrumentalism, I am concerned with redeeming the playful dimension of even those activities in which play and politics have been all but grounded by the demands of technology and the markets designed to serve it. If our ingenious calculations and computations have brought us to the present state of affairs, an appreciation of playfulness should break the fixations of the present, open routes to the past, and extend our future.

ENDEAVORING TO DEPART from the instrumentalism central to the culture of modernity, I would hope to express myself as fully as my friends, neighbors, publishers, readers, and critics will tolerate. Clearly, mine is a balancing act of sorts—an effort to communicate weighty matters lightly enough to entice others to join in. To stay in circulation, I am recollecting things I have stumbled across—the dual meanings of metaphors, that fork in the road which punctures a tire. Aiming no higher, I follow postmodernist practices, assume the risks of irony, and accept my paranoia as rational norm. Thus my overdeveloped, inflated sense of the oppressiveness of the present should allow me and others to enter that unreal, theatrical world in which changes in perception are sufficient for remaining composed.

Even as an eleven-year-old, a decade before the firebombing of my hometown of Dresden, the boundaries for my playing were tightly drawn. Equipped with a bicycle, I was left quite free to cruise both through the city and through the surrounding countryside—but warned to steer clear of people: "Don't get involved." To be safe wherever I might travel, I was to remain detached—a child in an adult world, a Jew in Germany, a German in Oregon, an Oregonian in the Ivy League, an Ivy Leaguer in

---

[2] George Kateb, *Hannah Arendt* (Totowa, N.J.: Rowland & Allenheld, 1983), pp. 181–82.

Hawaii, an alien at the party, an outsider inside. I have been talking and writing, I now think, so as to gain admission to the dominant culture while still remaining free to cruise.

Because it is hard to give a measure of public respectability to living in a state of permanent crisis, I keep implying that *all* of us are irrevocably wounded, that there is no way out. If this apocalyptic postulate grossly exaggerates our condition, it may nonetheless serve to intensify one's resolve to amplify the present moment. Like the knowledge of the prospect that one will be hanged in the morning, it should serve, as has been said, to concentrate the mind during the night. It should validate my inquiry into what we might do in the meantime, here and now—in that meantime which is the only time we have in any case.

Making us aware of our distinctive interests, the knowledge of our impending end alerts us to the way we are needlessly submissive, pathologically distracted and preoccupied. It alerts us to the imposition of autonomous abstractions such as Success, of dispensable ideals and ontologies. It is this knowledge of our finitude which moves me to decenter the optimism and rationalism of the Enlightenment by installing a counter-progressive structure, a map for coping under contemporary conditions.

Like Erving Goffman, a social scientist who remained disconcertingly cool in his reports on how others present themselves in everyday life, I realize that "he who would combat false consciousness and awaken people to their true interests has much to do, because their sleep is very deep." Yet I also believe that it is not enough, as he said, "merely to sneak in and watch the way people snore."[3] Troubled by those who merely take note of others—of Otherness outside and within ourselves—I would also have us arouse our dormant interests. I would have us transact our affairs with others so explicitly that the note-taking process itself becomes a form of politics, that is, an activity which provides a communal basis for enduring despite the forces which diminish us.

I assume that such performances will not change the waves which pound us. They are but a reaching for the kind of steady lucidity which I am at pains to read into the purposefulness of artists and children, of

---

[3] Erving Goffman, *Frame Analysis: An Essay on the Organization of Experience* (Cambridge: Harvard University Press, 1974), p. 14.

whoever is pounded by reality and yet capable of making light of his or her experience. Such purposefulness seems to me least adulterated in the activities of individuals who keep recollecting whatever has befallen them, who keep recalling and reviving whatever has broken their toys, their loves, their convictions. Forever scanning the horizon, careful not to focus too narrowly, they have learned to become secret agents, veritable Doppelgänger who keep equivocating and digressing so as to save the past and make it present. Because they continuously reframe their experiences and reenact their lives, I would wish to follow them so as to compose myself even while realizing that there is no way out, that we are inescapably circling, forever recycling what we encounter. Thus mine is but a strategy for encountering others and welcoming them in our assemblages and books. Within such shelters I would seek to include the dead and the unborn, to arouse and redeem the unlived lives within ourselves.

Of course this is scarcely the historical moment for celebrating such openness. The everything-is-permitted nihilism which triumphed in Hitler's Germany continues to haunt and paralyze us. To think of challenging and enlarging liberalism's model for living is to raise the specter of nihilism, of boundless permissiveness. To speak of de-creating, de-mythologizing, de-constructing, de-regulating, de-composing, de-idealizing, and de-sublimating and then to consecrate nothing firmer than unfocused cruising for integrating the angels and demons who encircle us is surely to retreat. Doesn't my discursive meandering question the glories of the Enlightenment, the progress we've made, the success that is almost ours, the light at the end?

When it dawns on us that playful behavior will certainly not reconstitute our lives, we shed our distinctively human character—our playfulness—and despair of art and artifice, duplicity and politics. Subduing the angel who guards the garden, we abandon our fictions and return to the state of pure reality. Ceasing to see the present moment as incomplete, we stop looking behind and thinking ahead. Instead, we are wholly filled by that kind of divine love for the authenticity of things—the whole of creation—which is quite unaware of itself, a love that Eve dismissed when she became excited by the serpent and flirtatiously, playfully began what has turned out to be man's venture—that agonizing down-to-earth drama in which women and men still have time to participate.

The Desperate Politics of Postmodernism

INTRODUCTION

IN THE contemporary world, despair rising out of boredom is the luxury of the privileged. Why, C. P. Cavafy has asked, are they going back home so lost in thought?

> What does this uneasiness mean,
> and this confusion? (How grave the faces have become!)
> Why are the streets and squares rapidly emptying,
> and why is everyone going back home so lost in thought?[1]

In the privileged parts of the world, the most agreeable of routines—commuting, working, shopping—extinguish consciousness of suffering, brutality, and death while giving rise to a nostalgia for frontier hardship and individual heroism. Of course, the prevailing uneasiness has not gone unnoticed. In the late 1970s President Jimmy Carter's doleful speech on America's pervasive malaise served as but another irritating reminder, one promptly disregarded by an electorate welcoming the buoyancy of the

---

[1] C. P. Cavafy, "Waiting for the Barbarians," in *Six Poets of Modern Greece*, trans. Edmund Keeley and Philip Sherrard (New York: Knopf, 1960).

Reagan administration. The malaise speech, as it came to be called, had actually been inspired by Christopher Lasch's reflections on "the culture of narcissism," which Lasch related to the flatness of American life:

> Today Americans are overcome not by the sense of endless possibility but by the banality of the social order they have erected against it. Having internalized the social restraints by means of which they formerly sought to keep possibility within civilized limits, they feel themselves overwhelmed by annihilating boredom, like animals whose instincts have withered in captivity. A reversion to savagery threatens them so little that they long precisely for a more vigorous instinctual existence.[2]

Yet how might "a more vigorous institutional existence" be brought about? After all, Lasch's words—my words as well—are colored by the very culture they lament. We can scarcely acknowledge that the source of our malaise resides within the agreeable setting which gives rise to our critical reflections. Suspecting the presence of some massive tumor and seeking its source, we encounter nothing definable, nothing comprehensible. There would appear to be no language for interrogating the status quo, no time or space for engaging in transactions that might redeem our everyday affairs.

Of course we have not yet come to the end of our days. Technology has not leveled the ups and downs of our lives. Looking in a mirror long enough, however, and looking for the worst, we do get intimations of ourselves as those automatons which Alexandre Kojève has seen to emerge at the end of history when "the species of Homo sapiens (which will live amidst abundance and complete security) will be content," when the species will "react by conditioned reflexes to vocal signals or sign 'language.' "[3] In this prophecy we are in the process of becoming functions of a larger system we neither know nor control. Everything becomes indiscriminately "normal"—simply the way it is. We fail to experience the satisfaction of *making* distinctions, of enacting our lives, of actualizing the

---

[2] Christopher Lasch, *The Culture of Narcissism* (New York: W. W. Norton, 1978), p. 11.

[3] Alexandre Kojève, *Introduction to the Reading of Hegel* (New York: Basic Books, 1969), pp. 160–61.

latent possibilities of our history. To be sure, we at present keep transforming our lives and the world. Yet increasingly our actions are unmediated reactions to a power that we neither direct nor organize, a power which possesses a vitality and an agenda quite its own. And where it is conspicuously displayed, as at world expositions, we eagerly stand in lines just to catch up with it.

What we come to experience, however, fails to surprise us. Although we spin the TV channel dial, the scene remains the same. We travel, but our destinations are as equivalent as the souvenirs from seemingly distant countries. Whatever we confront is readily reversible. As in the grid of telecommunications, space has disappeared between action and reaction, stimulus and response, input and output. Receivers *become* senders who *become* receivers. In the fictions of military strategists, arrival and departure become as synonymous as first strike and retaliation. A seamless meganetwork fuses alternative realities and eliminates the difference between preparation and execution. As the patterns we design to manage our experiences are dissolved, it becomes pointless to speak of successes and failures, beginnings and endings. We find ourselves strapped in a succession of preassigned seats in the midst of self-regulating, foolproof technologies. Once the loose ends of early space travel have been eliminated, once the Challenger's disastrous take-off has been eclipsed by the design of a flawless Challenger II, *anyone* can take the trip confident that all screws are self-adjusting. Once embarrassments like the former employers of G. Gordon Liddy or Oliver North have become anachronisms, all will be well.

Perceiving this future normality as partially realized in the present, we feel restless, wonder how this situation might have come about, and turn to historical narratives. How our routines make us irritable and finally subservient has been amply foretold and continues to be documented. We have become informed about quiet desperation in places where our technologies and bureaucracies have reduced the risk of everyday life, where both initiation rites and graduation exercises lack meaning, where insurance policies protect us against foul weather, where air-conditioning and frozen food have suspended the natural rhythms—the blessings and disasters—of the seasons. The diseases of modernism are so familiar that the names of their diagnosticians have become veritable icons: Marx, Dostoyevsky, Nietzsche, Durkheim, Henry Adams, Kierkegaard, Spengler, Sorel, Freud, Weber, Veblen, Mumford, Marcuse, Arendt, Solzhenitsyn, and Ellul. And lest we forge their analyses, we keep exposing ourselves to Kafka's stories, Godard's films, Bacon's paintings, Beattie's novels, Segal's sculptures, and Beckett's plays. Having enrolled in the proper book clubs and film societies, we ritualistically confirm how well prophecy and art show individuals to be broken up and trivialized by the division of their labor and the standardization of their experiences, to be alienated from their associates, from the products of their work, from whatever remains unmolested by the machine and its servants. Behind the disconnected scraps of their lives a self-generating and self-serving totality would seem to compute and define what is normal, useful, necessary, rational, efficient, and progressive. The energies unleashed by the Industrial Revolution are channeled by a postindustrial revolution, a control revolution which, as James R. Beniger has pointed out, shows no signs of abating. Three forces, he says, propel its development:

> First, energy utilization, processing speeds, and control technologies have continued to evolve in a positive spiral, advances in one sector causing—or at least enabling—improvements in the other two. Second, additional energy has increased not only the speed of material processing and transportation but their volume predictability as well. This, in turn, has further increased both the demand for control and the returns on new applications of information technology. Increases in the volume of production, for example, have brought additional advantages to increased consumption, which manufacturers have sought to control using the information technologies of market research and mass advertising. Similarly, the increased reliability of production and distribution flows has increased the economic returns on informational activities like planning, scheduling, and forecasting. Third, information processing and flows need themselves to be controlled, so that informational technologies must continue to be applied at higher and higher layers of control.[4]

John Kenneth Galbraith offers a terse projection:

---

[4] James R. Beniger, *The Control Revolution: Technological and Economic Origins of the Information Society* (Cambridge: Harvard University Press, 1986), pp. 433–34.

> Our wants will be managed in accordance "with the needs of the industrial system"; the policies of the state will be subject to similar influence; education will be adopted to industrial need; the disciplines required by the industrial system will be the conventional morality of the community. All other goals will be made to seem precious, unimportant or antisocial.[5]

AT THE END of the eighteenth century W. F. G. Hegel began to provide a metaphysical context within which Galbraith's as well as Kojève's reflections could flourish. It allowed him to prophesy that tendencies implicit in the process of modernization will engender a postmodernist universal state beyond all human history—that is, beyond all those agonizing contradictions, duplicities, and ironies which inspired the heroic acts that are the featured attraction of conventional historical narratives.[6] Within a posthistorical world (the one toward which underdeveloped nations are inexorably moving however much they want to do so under local management) an impersonal universal technicism will have come into its own and will pursue no end other than its own augmentation. Hegel's view if not his metaphysics was shared by a host of thinkers who saw the forces inaugurating humanity's posthistorical synthesis as fulfillment of the Industrial Revolution and the promise of the Enlightenment. Neither church nor state would stand in the way.

Clearly the politics of liberalism has been impotent in its confrontation with the dynamism it unleashed in the private sector by imposing

---

[5] John Kenneth Galbraith, *Economics and Public Purpose* (New York: New American Library, 1975), p. 405.

[6] Only a footnote more elaborate than this one can do justice to Barry Cooper's interpretation of Hegel via Alexandre Kojève—especially to Cooper's perception of multinational corporations, the Gulag camps, and technological nihilism as encompassed by Hegel's design. See *The End of History: An Essay on Modern Hegelianism* (Toronto: University of Toronto Press, 1984), chap. 8. Hegel's prophecy, it needs to be added, was considerably more complex than Kojève allowed; it provided not only for the integration of all Otherness within Reality but also for a phoenix arising from the ashes. On technical imperatives, also see Manfred Stanley, *The Technological Conscience* (Chicago: University of Chicago Press, 1978); William Kuhns, *The Post-Industrial Prophets: Interpretations of Technology* (New York: Weybright and Takkey, 1971); Herbert Marcuse, *One-Dimensional Man* (Boston: Beacon Press, 1964); and the various publications by George Grant. Also see the extensive references in Beniger, *The Control Revolution*, pp. 439–76.

constitutional constraints only on public government. To be sure, liberals such as John Locke, Adam Smith, and James Madison had no cause to worry about the unlimited industriousness of the private entrepreneur. They knew technology to be localized—certainly not primed to internationalize corporations, annex the planets, or change the genetic code. Nor did they anticipate that governmental institutions and the mass media would simply reinforce the process of industrialization and modernization. Permeating every sector of life, private interests were to become public except in name. By the 1980s the popularity of Reagan administration made clear that little more than an antitechnological nostalgia remained within the liberal state to check the impulse to expand, to use knowledge for the endless enhancement of man's power.

The nihilistic drive of the enterprises of modernity is accompanied by a massive forgetfulness. In the 1970s Langdon Winner published a study (subtitled "technics out of control") which interpreted Mary Shelley's *Frankenstein, or The Modern Prometheus* (1818) as an account of the way scientific ingenuity and utilitarian rationality leads to a kind of amnesia, a loss of an ecological consciousness:

> Frankenstein is a person who discovers, but refuses to ponder, the implication of his discovery. He is a man who creates something new in the world and then pours all of his energy into an effort to forget. His invention is incredibly powerful and represents a quantum jump in the performance capability of a certain kind of technology. Yet he sends it out into the world with no real concern for how best to include it in the human community. . . . Provided with no plan for its existence, the technological creation enforces a plan upon its creator. . . . Technology allows us to ignore our own works. It is *license to forget.*[7]

Unsymbolized—Dr. Frankenstein's monster itself remained nameless—technological creations are simply brute reality—uncomprehended, anonymous forces. Radically alien, they give point to Gertrude Stein's remark that some things which are there (she was referring to Oakland, California) are not there. Seeking to take our bearings, we sense the vacuity at the

---

[7] Langdon Winner, *Autonomous Technology* (Cambridge: M.I.T. Press, 1977), pp. 313, 315.

center of the technological structures surrounding us. There is no distinctive moment at which someone—someone present—might actually decide what to do or not to do, whether or not to push the button to activate the latest generation of nuclear weapons. There are no discrete acts: to prepare to strike is but part of the process of striking. The end is implicit in the beginning. There may be those two proverbial missile-activating buttons and two leaders to give orders to push them. But within a seamless process they are pushed by dispassionate "individuals" who themselves are pushed by the rationality that inheres in their knowledge that the species is finally saved only in a process that terminates it. A comprehensive rationality makes an offensive first strike identical to a defensive preemptive strike which has been quite rationally prepared so as to prevent an offensive first strike which has been quite rationally prepared so as to bring the machinery of death into being. In this momentum time dissolves. The concept of duration becomes meaningless. If we still feel ourselves to be present and in control, this is only insofar as we actively contribute to the thrust of prevailing installations. If we are still conscious and mindful at the end, our final *act* can only be to outperform an otherwise self-enacting reality. The challenge and excitement of extinguishing ourselves is all that keeps us alive. In the words of the director of the nuclear weapons program at Los Alamos, "At present, both in offensive uses as well as defense, the program is more exciting than I've ever known it."[8]

DURING THE TIME between awareness and repression of this deadly logic—this wholly rational madness, this wholly mad rationality—we search for escapes. As history unfolds or, in Hegel's terms, fulfills and consumes itself, we seek that secure center which still holds, that sane, sensible ground on which we might manage to rally, to pull the pieces together, to communicate. Near desperation, we yearn for a viable foundation somewhere—some ground on which to give expression for our true selves outside the prevailing disorder. We scan self-help manuals and run marathons in the hope of reaching the one good place—the perfect place to settle, the place to be at rest. Yet as we seek to detach ourselves from the centers of technological power, we do not travel lightly; we

[8] Paul Robinson, quoted in *International Herald Tribune,* March 31, 1986, p. 4.

remain burdened by our awareness of the dubiousness of our quests. Muckraking and deconstructionism have left their mark, irritating us as we dream of abandoning not only the technological grid but the society that sustains it, as we hope somehow to become self-sufficient, to be neither buyer nor seller, neither administrator nor administered. While hankering for a life without dependencies or commitments, we stay in our careers and buy recreational vehicles. Even as we manage to break out, we remain implicated in our instrumentalism, think of the *uses* of the wilderness, and calculate the costs and benefits of roughing it for a weekend in the woods. Our escapes, too, remain utilitarian. In quest of space where we might redesign our lives, we go with the very equipment, both intellectual and mechanical, which keeps us arrested where we are. Programming ourselves to be rational, we believe that we must *first* define our objectives and *then* work to achieve them. We carry with us an orientation in which techniques are separated from goals: if we but perfect our techniques we will assuredly arrive. Thus although we may aim high—zero population growth, self-sufficient communes, a deschooled and dehospitalized society, or the minimalist aesthetics implicit in the ideology that small is beautiful—our steady focus on the means for getting there keeps us grounded.

And on the ground our restlessness remains. Looking for goods—unambiguous goods—we realize that our cars or foods or appliances are less satisfying than the background against which they are displayed in magazine ads: an untraveled country road, a farmhouse kitchen, a family dinner, a joyous party. Our ideal landscape is pastoral, our best tools old and simple. We would like to withdraw to green sanctuaries which protect us against reckless appetites and driving passions. On guard against the dangers of extremism—the loss of self either through surrender to others or victory over them—we feel that life is best when friendship is easy, religion bland, and language soothing. Equanimity is promised by half-hour workouts, burnished furniture, a house at the seashore, meditation between appointments, and a politics of apathy. As the excitements of narcissism turn into indolence, we cherish scenes that are candle lit, pillow furnished, and snug. Sliding toward inaction, we silently space out and pulsate in unison. No ordeals, no pain. We come to an end—and yet it is an end which some nagging, secret part of us still wants to leave. Like

Dostoyevsky's underground man, we seem to want no peace—no retreat that would at last *satisfy* our needs. Even when the flawless calculator of pleasure designed by Jeremy Bentham and B. F. Skinner assures us that things are going well we feel the impulse to complicate our existence. We anxiously scan the landscape and dream of escaping the merchants of nostalgia, the unrelenting utilitarianism of the age.

No public ground for sustaining a viable alternative being available, we remain impotent and lonely, at best displaying what John Updike has called the bleak dignity of solitude. Sensing no shared ground as we probe alternative possibilities, our acts of resistance are meager, private, frivolous, incoherent. Worse, they seem scarcely defensible:

> Men play with one another in bars around a few beers, a game of darts or a game of pool. Others go to the races or play cards. As among women, social contact is mediated by a common activity that resembles the play of childhood but is presented in the form of "games" in which the object is to win money, since there are few other circumstances in which men are prepared to confess that an activity is, in itself, engrossing. They cannot admit the legitimacy of play, even as they enact this need spontaneously in barroom encounters or the formation of voluntary social clubs. Some of these social clubs exist as veterans' organizations, civic groups, or fraternal groups of ethnically homogenous persons who require support in the transition to the new society. In these instances, the need for fraternity is masked as participation in public life, but its real substance is the hunger for communication and social interaction.[9]

As Stanley Aronowitz observes, even in after-hours activities "mere" play is treated as instrumental. A sovereign instrumentalism reduces impulses through which brute reality may be redefined and decentered.

But where can we locate a community that deflects the imposition of finalities, that treats all forces impinging on us—including those created

---

[9] Stanley Aronowitz, *False Promises: The Shaping of American Working Class Consciousness* (New York: McGraw-Hill, 1973), pp. 92--93. That novelists and short story writers keep identifying the private space in which a minimal politics persists is shown by Elizabeth Long, *The American Dream and the Popular Novel* (Boston: Routledge & Kegan Paul, 1985); see also Carol Anshaw, "Fiction in the Passive Voice," *Village Voice Literary Supplement*, October 1986, pp. 12–13.

by ourselves—as *un*real? Where can we find models for opposing the forces which destroy our relations with one another, with the products of our work, with our past and our future? Where can we connect with the forces of destruction—the sublime, spectacular Death we project—and bring them into our communities?

Shortly before Rilke died of a form of leukemia whose last stages were painful and disfiguring, he refused the comfort of drugs so as to protect that time and space in which he might relate to his experience. He wrote a young poet:

> Death is the side of life which is turned away from us, and upon which we shed no light. We must try to widen our consciousness of existence so that it is at home in both spheres, with no dividing-line between them, so that we may draw endless sustenance from both. The true way of life leads through both kingdoms, the great circulation of the blood passes through both: there is neither a here nor a hereafter but a single great unity.[10]

Yet in what time and space can our consciousness include the Otherness in our lives? What models for decentering technology remain available?

---

[10] Rainer Maria Rilke, *Letters to a Young Poet* (New York: Random House, 1984).

1 ART IN PROCESS

BREAKS in our routines—accidents, calamities, holidays, or mere coffee breaks—give us intimations of a dimension of existence that contradicts the instrumentalism which consumes us. When these intimations also give us pause, our private fantasies unfold. Repressed feelings rise to the surface and come into play. During such intervals we may welcome impulses which, once admitted, divert us further from the task at hand. We make idle gestures and suddenly value gratuitous digressions from necessity. Inexplicably, we feel more whole—more engaged. Indifferent to the distinction between means and ends, we inhabit a clearing that is open to alien interests, that entices outsiders to extend our play.

In such clearings we engage in the politics of those eighteenth-century Americans who had assembled on newly captured territory to keep the ends of life uncongealed by devising a system of checks and balances. Today it is harder to persist in their effort, for the framers of the American constitution hardly foresaw how an ascending technology would serve to consolidate society and induce us to comply with our schedules. They did not anticipate how effectively technology would define the limits of rational conduct through the school system, the mass media, and ubiquitous artifacts such as assembly lines, communication grids, shopping malls, and office buildings.[1] While their constitutional politics may continue to check and balance official, public government, it can scarcely cope with the economic and industrial forces which, eagerly served by educational, scientific, and cultural establishments, structure the rest of American life.[2]

Nonetheless artistic enterprises, while no less subservient to technology and its market, are unlike others insofar as they keep calling attention to their own procedures. They thereby display the very process articulated by America's eighteenth-century politicians who had resolved to block whatever forces might oppress the nation's citizens. Thus to take full account of artistic enterprises is to become aware of a politics which disrupts and pluralizes an all-too homogenized society. It is to perceive what it means to be actors engaged in public affairs that serve no purpose other than maintaining the arena for performing, whose sole concern it is to keep the play going, to postpone the closing of the curtain.

As the contemporary artist abandons the modernists' hope of overcoming the structures of modern life, she (or he) brings repressed interests into public view by explicitly including her false starts and wayward impulses in her projects. Not embarrassed to place the process of production on exhibit, she leaves it to others to distinguish between conception, rehearsal, performance, and recollection. Not framing the parts of her work—work which itself is barely framed—she leaves room in which others—Otherness—can establish what her subject matter excludes. By thus including what she seems to brush aside, she deprives her end product of its definitiveness, and hence of the artist's power to overwhelm and deactivate. Conveying more, she imposes less. And because she does so quite explicitly she allows us to identify a discipline—a politics—which is at once expressive and inclusive.

---

[1] On the organizing power of cultural artifacts, see Langdon Winner, "Do Artifacts Have Politics?" *Daedalus* 109 (Winter 1980): 121–36.

[2] The marginality of political institutions in "normalizing" American life is reviewed in works ranging from C. Wright Mills's *The Power Elite* (1956) to William E. Connolly's *The Politics of Ambiguity* (1988).

Particularly in their minimalist, conceptualist form, the contemporary arts have been treating settled structures of experience as unsettled, unending processes. Dissolving the so-called reality of a still life, a landscape, a human figure, or a relationship, they have allowed little to remain merely what it is said to be. And more than the scientific establishments and political institutions of industrial societies, the arts persist in seeking to enlist their public in their efforts to become detached from overpowering conceptual systems and deadening structures. As the artist treats heavy, solidified structures of experience lightly, she moves her audience out of its conventional frames and brings it into relation to new ones.

If the basic strategy of contemporary art is to *settle* for nothing, to shift into overdrive if necessary, it encourages placing whatever has become a fixed element of reality—a silent child, a can of soup, the day's job, a nursing home for the aged, the evening news—in an unfamiliar milieu, a new environment, an artist-designed context. The artist integrates a screeching sound into a familiar melody or, what is harder, creates a redeeming setting for the latest missile and, harder yet, eases what is full of the Otherness of death—Hiroshima or Little Big Horn or the forests of Vorkuta—into a coherent narrative. Yet, however hard it is to come to terms with the extremities of experience, her discipline demands the use of perspectives which integrate them, which add dimensions to whatever is assumed to be final.

IN *One Flew Over the Cuckoo's Nest* (1975), McMurphy (Jack Nicholson in the film based on Ken Kesey's book) shows what it takes to break out of a wearisome mental institution. After commandeering a bus and taking a dozen fellow inmates for a short ride to the seashore, he gives them courage to embark on a fishing trip. They seek to rent a boat, but its owner views them suspiciously. Without hesitation McMurphy introduces his motley crew as physicians—and instantly places them in a redeeming context. The boat owner (and we in the audience as well) experience a gestalt switch: they *are* physicians. Though it's not much of a revolution, the boundaries drawn around behavior labeled "psychotic" and "normal" have changed. More: we are delighted as suddenly everything is at risk once reality is deprived of inherent properties and structures, centers and limits, causes and consequences, plots and sequences.

McMurphy and his fellow inmates have taken a small step toward that unbearable state of permanent crisis in which nothing is real and everything is critical, in which we continuously agonize how to maintain our balance. No wonder the panel of all-too-real doctors who meet to diagnose McMurphy recoil from such a state. They regard him as "incurably antisocial"—as insensitive to the all-too-human need for law and order. If we are nonetheless attracted by McMurphy's risky histrionics, this is because we are sharing the excitement of efforts to reconstruct the meaning of reality. And while *One Flew over the Cuckoo's Nest* is no timeless classic, neither are our own quests for transforming our lives.

Jack Nicholson as McMurphy begins his act precisely where he had been grounded by court order—within a dull, lifeless cuckoo's nest. No grand strategist with global ambitions, he seeks no more than to embrace his apathetic fellow inmates and to lead them into a somewhat larger world. A steady talker in need of stimulation and company, he questions the heavy routines of his immediate surroundings and lets light flood in. His every move is a reality-agitating provocation, a sly, equivocal, playful courting of hard-and-fast finalities. Although he signally declines to court the head nurse—she so enrages him that he loses his cool, and going for her throat, seals his own end—all his other acts are those of the lover who risks failure, whose mere glance expresses an expectation, whose very posture of expectancy is a turn-on. His is a precarious, tireless effort to detach his companions from their preoccupations, to make them participate in his life, ultimately to involve them as confederates and fellow players. Until his arrival, they had been passively absorbed by their routines. But once he has cleared space in which they can act, they do not want the music to stop and the dance to end.

The participatory democratic thrust of Nicholson's act has been clearly expressed by Arthur Sainer's *Radical Theater Notebook* (1975). Sainer notes that the moment so-called reality is perceived as unreal—as the unreal world of the theater—the spectator starts to participate. He is

> given the chance to physically test out the illusory figures performing for him and to discover that these figures may be no more illusory than he himself is, may be realer than he, may in fact be fraudulent, may be neither illusory nor symbolic at all but nervous, vibrating, questioning creatures who, like himself—the spectator—are trying to find their way in the play.

> The spectator in the radical theatre may be finding something that the play has been unable to find before his appearance on the scene. As the play breaks down many of the barriers between life and art, the spectator may find out something about his life through his physical entrance into art.[3]

In the unreal world of art, spectator-actors keep shifting their angle of vision—probing, teasing, taunting, agitating, abusing, and traumatizing whatever emerges as oppressively real. Looking at the world askew, they conduct experiments in derangement.

GLANCING BEYOND DOMINANT arrangements, the artist allows his belief in reality to dissolve until he can scarcely manage to steady himself. He takes risks and goes against the odds. He stops calculating and cost-accounting. Contradicting the ordinary consistencies of diction and behavior, he escapes those automatic happy-day-wishing chants that fail to loosen the dark knots inside ourselves. In the process of surrendering all but his consciousness to unmanaged experience, the artist proceeds to seize and consolidate what is happening to him. To the extent that he creates a setting that is more comprehensive than the reality which claims him, he succeeds where Hamlet failed. Hamlet, Eileen Jorge Allman has noted, fell short of consolidating and reconstructing his life because he could not view it comprehensively enough. The play he staged for exposing the corrupt members of the court to themselves, for making them feel their guilt, had not brought them into a larger order of being: "In leaping at the opportunity to demonstrate his own awareness and thus unburden himself of the vices and guilts that he carries within himself for his whole society, Hamlet moves prematurely into play. His part becomes the medium for personal release *but not the medium of social redemption*."[4] His play exposed the raw nerves of passion of the court, but because it did no more it led to disaster. True, his fixed self-image had dissolved; he had managed to drop his defenses and release the demons within him. But the *form* of his play, its genre, failed to dissolve the frozen images of those who surrounded him.

---

[3] Arthur Sainer, *The Radical Theater Notebook* (New York: Avon, 1975), p. 79.

[4] Eileen Jorge Allman, *Player-King and Adversary* (Baton Rouge: Louisiana State University Press, 1980), pp. 234–35 (my emphasis).

The artist's discipline—his controlled playfulness—consists not only of breaking boundaries but also of implicating others (arrested parts of himself) in his efforts to manage an enlarged range of experience. "It's all about risks, deliberate risks," Helen Frankenthaler has reflected on her own work as painter; "the picture unfolds, leads, unravels as I push ahead. Watching it develop, *I seize it*."[5] Allowing the subject of her work to fascinate and lead her, the artist not only forges ahead but also remains in the human community. Others accompany her. She gives them (and herself) the reassurance of props, landmarks, maps, expectations. She provides subjects and implies they are meaningful. While she encourages reality to become transparent and risks her very identity in the process, she pauses for breath. She constructs frameworks and shelters.

Yet as she and her fellow players weary of their shelter, she again begins to break the rules that make it comfortable. She invents new ones that give credence to exceptions, to conceptual overflow. While she crosses the boundaries of venerable structures—a stage or a museum, a prison or a hospital—she accepts old melodies, time-worn plots, and tired wayfarers. As she moves ahead she abandons neither her past nor her surroundings. Her posture is sketched with stunning precision in Whitman's *Song of Myself:*

> Apart from the pulling and hauling stands what I am,
> Stands amused, complacent, compassionate, idle, unitary,
> Looks down, is erect, or bends an arm on an impalpable
> certain rest,
> Looking with side-curved head curious what will come next,
> Both in and out of the game and watching and wondering
> at it.

Both in and out she's a savior of sorts, a member of a community which constitutes the only ground she knows for transforming passions into the filigree of love letters, fragments of experience into biographies, the life and death of the homeless into narratives.

Like Socrates inviting his friends to leave the city, amble toward the

---

[5] Helen Frankenthaler, quoted in Karen Wilkin, *Frankenthaler: Works on Paper 1949–84* (New York: Braziller, 1985).

hills, and ultimately scale new heights, the artist keeps departing from what is close at hand. He starts in the midst of ordinary affairs and draws attention to some inarticulate element which contradicts the surface of our life: a festering wound, an unremembered dream, an impulse to kill. He makes out-of-sight experience visible, says what had gone without saying. Relating it, he comes to terms with alien dimensions of himself and his society. He domesticates it.

To be sure, his neighbors may remain unmoved by him, remaining behind like Socrates's companions. They may be comfortable seeing an urban riot, an apathetic child, or a chance meeting in quite conventional terms. For them, life is no more than it's said to be by those empowered to name things. They are content to leave things the way they're said to be and do not wish to ask for more. "So it goes," they are then apt to conclude without irony. They want no further trouble.

And in the end, the artist may retreat. Agreeing that no additional dimensions and no alternative futures are conceivable, he may allow himself to be caught up in irreducibly brute experience. He may grant that pain and pleasure are what they are: life is for real. As long, however, as he can live life deliberately and envisage alternatives, he will be at play. He will disengage and reengage himself—not sequentially (as my language unavoidably implies) but in unified acts.

Sitting on a bench in a public park, I witness what seems to be a chance meeting of a woman and a man. Is it really a chance meeting? Might they not be lovers? Elaborating on the ordinary, I see more. Redefining the situation, giving a "chance meeting" a new context, I set aside conventional rules of evidence designed to keep me from imagining things. I change the rules so as to divert myself. Becoming "unrealistic," I am guided by Antonioni's comment on his film making: "We know that under the image revealed there is another which is truer to reality and under this image still another and yet again still another under this one perhaps right down to the decomposition of any reality."[6] Unlike the protagonist of Antonioni's *Blow-Up* I have no camera to document the meeting I witness. Yet I too focus on what I see. Becoming more imaginative, I enact

---

[6] Michelangelo Antonioni, quoted in Charles Thomas Samuels, *Encountering Directors* (New York: G. P. Putman's Sons, 1972), p. 23.

increasingly more of my fantasy, enlist others to enact my play. Even more ambitiously, I seek financial backing so as to recruit a veritable network of actors. Cajoled and inspired and remunerated by me, won't they accept my fiction, contribute to it, and act convincingly? Actors all, might they not finally *make* a scene and appear on nothing less than the stage of history?

Limited only by my resources for imagining and financing a scenario powerful enough to persuade me and others of the reality of my allegations, I come to realize—to know—precisely how fully we can act. And I will *know* how much history we enacted the moment we're exhausted, ignored, exiled, or destroyed. We will have joined the company of picaros, confidence men, double agents, imposters, charlatans, jesters, actors, and players—whoever has elicited performances from the repressed elements of life and moved closer to making alternatives real, closer to knowing and realizing them.

IN 1966 ROBERT Venturi inverted the austere modernism of Le Corbusier's and Miës van der Rohe's structures by arguing for a more inclusive architecture. "More is not less," he wrote. And further: "An architecture of complexity and contradiction has a special obligation toward the whole; its truth must be in its totality." He elaborated as if touched by Walt Whitman: "I like elements which are hybrid rather than pure. . . . I am for messy vitality over obvious unity. . . . I prefer 'both-and' to 'either-or.' "[7] Made bored, apprehensive, or anxious by the stuffiness of conventional wisdom, Venturi and other postmodernist architects redesigned the world so that a messy vitality could make its appearance. In the same spirit, Symbolists had produced new forms to present disreputable subject matter while Dadaists had assembled "materials noble or looked down upon, verbal clichés or clichés of old magazines, bromides, publicity slogans, refuse, etc."[8] Their projects were designed, as John McDermott has noted, to incorporate "bits and pieces, some old, some new, some

---

[7] Robert Venturi, *Complexity and Contradiction in Architecture* (New York: Museum of Modern Art, 1977), p. 23.

[8] William C. Seitz, *The Art of Assemblage* (New York: Museum of Modern Art, 1961), p. 39.

thrown away, some kept out of nostalgia . . . [to] assemble a new environment and [to] return life and meaning to these fragments."[9] Collages and assemblages—like the revisionist histories of feminists—were to give vitality to discarded and ignored aspects of life—to rejects, castaways, fugitives. Kurt Schwitter's famous Merzbau, a huge combination of house, sculpture, and unclassified brick-a-brack (destroyed in the last days of World War II yet preserved in photographs) was an effort to salvage the dead scraps of modern life.[10] Similarly August Strindberg, as Donald Burnham has noted, treated nothing as marginal when walking through the streets of the Montparnasse section of Paris. In the course of his lonely walks he found meaning everywhere:

> Flowers in the Luxembourg Gardens seemed to nod at him, sometimes in greeting, sometimes in warning. Clouds in the shape of animals foretold ominous events. Statues looked at him trying to tell him something. Scraps of paper in the gutter carried words that he tried to piece together into a message. Books which he found in sidewalk bookstalls seemed to have been specially "placed" there for him. The design of a leather cover of one seemed to contain a prophecy for him and when he opened the book a sliver of wood pointed to a particular sentence. Twigs on the ground took the shape of the initials of a man who he feared was pursuing him intent on murder.[11]

Such accommodations—constructions—treat nothing as excessive or extraneous. The artist's very signature, her imprint, is part of the composition. Encouraging *all* elements to participate, she declines to attend to only one thing at a time. Breaking things up (as in Cubism) or creating a sense of immediacy by making foreground and background equally sharp (as in Photorealism or superrealist short stories), she illuminates unfamiliar aspects of familiar experience. As Tom Wolfe has said about the New Journalism, the artist records "everyday gestures, habits,

---

[9] John McDermott, *The Culture of Experience* (New York: New York University Press, 1976), p. 95.

[10] See John Elderfield, *Kurt Schwitters* (New York: Thames & Hudson, 1985).

[11] Donald L. Burnham, "Strindberg's Inferno and Sullivan's 'Extravasation of Meaning,'" *Contemporary Psychoanalysis* 9 (1973): 191–92.

manners, customs, styles of furniture, clothing, decoration, styles of traveling, eating, keeping house, modes of behaving toward children, servants, superiors, inferiors, peers."[12] A voracious, Godlike leveler, she seeks to take it all in. However she may depict the world, she perceives the visual field like a seasoned soccer or chess player—in a single unfocused glance. Treating figure and ground with serene impartiality, she shares Flaubert's yearning for a work so limpid that the flow of experience stands revealed in its totality:

> What seems beautiful to me, what I should like to write, is a book about nothing, a book dependent on nothing external, which would be held together by the internal strength of its style, just as the earth, suspended in the void, depends on nothing external for its support; a book which would have almost no subject, or at least in which the subject would be almost invisible.[13]

As the artist's expressions approach the flow of the barest of gestures, the specific content of his work loses in conventional meaning; his work serves to de-idealize its subject matter, its very creator. He may fail in this, as Marcel Duchamp learned when his ready-mades became celebrated icons ("nobody's perfect," he said with a shrug after his bottle drying rack was sold). Yet he persisted, engaging in automated drawing so that his products could betray no more authentic meaning than the work of the potter whose hand is not guided by his mind, who frustrates the impulse to conform to dated notions of perfection. Such projects, however variously they fail, deflate rational plans. They desublimate imperious monuments and thereby allow unaccredited elements at the edge of consciousness to flood in. They efface the subject and dismiss the artist. Confronting Robert Barry's photographs which claim to record the invisible movement of gases released into the air, we are moved to ask, "What is it, why do I look at it, and what am I doing here?" We are moved to raise the same question by Ad Reinhardt's attempts during his last period as

---

[12] Tom Wolfe, *The New Journalism* (New York: Harper & Row, 1973), p. 32.

[13] Gustave Flaubert, letter to Louise Colet, in Francis Steegmuller, ed. and trans., *The Letters of Gustave Flaubert: 1830–1857* (Cambridge: Harvard University Press, 1980), p. 154.

painter to disestablish art and put nothing in its place. Producing variations of black paintings, he proclaimed that they were about nothing. Free from all associations, they were devoid, Reinhardt insisted, of all meaning.[14] In the same spirit, Robert Barry announced formally that "during the exhibition the gallery will be closed,"[15] and Robert Morris created a construction to which he attached a notarized statement affirming that he was its maker, that he nevertheless withdrew all aesthetic claims for it, and that "from the date hereof said construction has no quality and content." A park warden in Tanzania, Myles Turner, went further: "I've had enough. I loved hunting, I've shot ever since I was a kid, but you go on killing these animals and all this misery gets to you. You just get through it, and there comes the stage when you want to do something for the animals, and then you get mad on photography. And the final stage is to sit in your car, without your camera or anything and just look at them."[16]

Such dismantlements of clear focal points are but an extension of the artist's hard-won indifference to what is deemed appropriate subject matter. Junk finds a place in Joseph Cornell's boxes and Robert Rauschenberg's combines. Debris, discards, ready-mades, and pop artifacts are made parts of compositions and finally make their way into museums. Nothing would seem to contain this process. Subverting the integrity of museums, there are video tapes, firework displays, sky writing, blade lighting, and performance art which offer nothing worth mentioning in aesthetic discourse—even as the Nothing the artist offers may come to be framed, criticized, cataloged, and merchandized. His posture is one of disarming indecisiveness. Making his appearances, he would appear to have no desires, no expectations. His paint drips, his words flow. His expressions seem slapdash, shapeless, and careless. Using crumbled fenders or driftwood, he will not discriminate. Rejecting epiphonemas and climaxes, moving toward no resolutions, his work remains open to acci-

---

[14] See *Art-as-Art: The Selected Writings of Ad Reinhardt* (New York: Viking, 1975). Also see Lucy R. Lippard, *Ad Reinhardt* (New York: Abrams, 1981).

[15] Robert Barry, "Closed Gallery," card from galleries in Amsterdam, Turin, Los Angeles, and Mary Boone Gallery (1981).

[16] Myles Turner, quoted in Harold T. P. Hayes, "The Last Place," *New Yorker*, December 6, 1976, p. 78.

dents, random events, happenings. Within a timeless omnipresent—the continuous present tense of the short story—he presumes no stable point of view from which to recollect the past or project the future. In a process of scanning and browsing he moves serendipidously in opposition to computer-aided searches for unambiguously relevant material. His projects fail to provide that "controlling idea" which art appreciation courses teach us to look for. As Hilton Kramer anxiously noted in his review of the Chicago Art Institute's "Europe in the Seventies," such art provides no durable works. It leaves art historians and art critics with little more than documents, photographs, items of hardware, and bibliographies. What it does present, Kramer wrote with dismay, has "so little visual interest that we know at once that the real center of this art lies elsewhere, in some realm outside the boundaries of visual experience, which is a very odd place, of course, for visual art to be."[17]

And, of course, it *is* an odd place—an unsettled and unsettling realm in which, it would seem, anything can happen. "Acceptance of the accidental is a work of artistic confidence," John Updike has observed, adding that he knows

> a painter who, having placed his easel, declines all further options of selectivity and renders onto canvas every detail before him. I know a writer who finds it difficult to conceive of situations, incidents, or even names different from those which actually cohered in a nexus of facts that momentarily generated the electricity and resonance of the "fictional." Every moment is, in a sense, a dealt hand. The combinations that the human mind invents are relatively facile and unmagical compared to reality's tumbling richness. Behind the artist's transformative sorcery lurks, like a sheepish apprentice, an irrational willingness to view the accidents of the actual as purposeful and the given as sacred. We are all artists insofar as we take the inexorable and quite unchosen data of our own circumstances and philosophically internalize them, give them a significance to match their awful centrality and thus lend our lives a "meaning."[18]

---

[17] Hilton Kramer, "Art in Chicago: Europe Avant-Garde Offers Little for the Eye," *International Herald Tribune,* October 8–9, 1977, p. 7.

[18] John Updike, "Card Tricks," *New Yorker,* April 18, 1977, p. 156.

We are all artists, Updike says, when we refrain from imposing "the combinations the human mind invents," when our own expressions are but exercises in restraint, invitations to the world to express itself. Thus even at its most withdrawn, in the form of minimalism, art is expressive—expressive of a determination to hear the endless claims of alien forces. Art elaborates on our journeys—manifestly so in Richard Long's arrangements that are but maps, photographs, and diagrams of his hikes through the countryside, none pointing to a destination. As he deprives pre-established landmarks and milestones of authority, unseen odds and ends emerge. A language which moves relentlessly in a linear, consequential way toward truth is demoted in favor of expressions that encourage the appearance of vagrants and castaways. Conversation takes over and displaces the quest for truth. Asides become central. The Platonist tradition of logocentrism is eclipsed, and it becomes possible to rehabilitate talking and telling, singing and pausing, to provide for that meandering vernacular discourse which is exiled by the spirit of fastidious exactitude. The environment enters and we can appreciate Hebrew or Latin without understanding a word. Allowing for the cadence, tone, shading, timbre, and pacing excluded by ourselves as binary word processors, more of the world finds a place in our lives. Our hands, too, become parts of speech. Oral poetry, like jazz, given resonance to hesitancies, interludes, pauses, inflections, and emphases, to affirmations barely hinted at by spaces between paragraphs, punctuation marks, musical notations, or italics. At the moment that conception, composition, and execution are integrated, the artist enacts both past and future. In a process that culminates in a structure of her design, she will have succeeded in framing forces which had been out of control.

2 TRANSACTIONAL AESTHETICS

HOWEVER relentlessly the artist breaks her (or his) obsessions and reassembles the pieces, she proceeds hesitantly, obliquely, experimentally. Her caution is understandable, for as she strikes out for new territory she risks losing the comforts of the old. Worse, the new structures she places into the world may turn out to be as oppressive as those she has transformed. Proceeding reluctantly, she will neither go all the way nor go for broke. She follows Whitman's effort to engage in nothing more than a form of guessing:

> For it is not what I have put into it that I
> have written this book,
> Nor is it by reading it you will acquire it . . .
> For all is useless without that which you may
> guess at many times and not hit, that which I
> hinted at. . . . [1]

---

[1] Walt Whitman, "Whoever You Are Holding Me Now in Hand," *Leaves of Grass* (1860).

It is the artist's diffidence—her reserve—which induces readers and spectators and audiences to start guessing, to articulate their interests, and to encounter the unfamiliar. Thus Christo's "Wrapped Coast" (1969), "Valley Curtain" (1970–1972), and "Running Fence" (1977), although providing disruptive structures, imposed nothing that lasted even as they activated financiers, contractors, attorneys, merchants, and publicists who identified their interest in the process of joining the artist by responding to his performance.

The activating participatory thrust of artworks is exemplified by Maya Ying Lin's Vietnam Veterans Memorial in Washington, D.C., the most frequently visited site in the capital. Unlike its fashionable monumental counterpart erected nearby (three soldiers in battle dress) the Memorial's reticence implicates visitors and releases emotions in a way tellingly described by Elizabeth Talent:

> The wings of the Memorial were visible on either side, for it is shaped like a long, open hinge, its leaves cut vertically into the ground, which descends very gradually toward the vertex, the effect as you come near being a little like facing a huge open book with black pages, just over ten feet high, that embrace you in a barely perceptible angle and slant away as gleaming walls for about eighty yards. . . .
>
> I descended slightly, almost imperceptibly—the rim of grass now at my knees, now my thighs, as if I waded into water—reading as I went, for the long, long quadrangle bore lines of names. The names had, like any such list, a great, provocative power. A list is an excerpt from reality, pure data that haven't been tampered with, and as Americans we trust such excerpted reality, we almost instinctively treat it with seriousness—we like the propriety of sheer information. In a way, it's what we're at home with. A list seems to represent a face of reality which is, for once, candid and free of emotional clutter; it's a kind of virgin territory. In a way, we wish to believe that our own perceptions are sufficiently good, clear-eyed, and sound, that our interpretation of the data, not someone else's, is what matters, and the closer we are to the unmanipulated, undoctored source the better—the greater the likelihood that some truth will be obtained. This is democratic. It's American to distrust incantations and obscurities, to want to go straight to the heart of the matter. That, I thought, was partly why this list inscribed

in black granite had such power: because in the nimble shifts of syllables, constantly compounded, in the rhythm of the names, first, middle, and last, first, middle and last, and in the sparks the names struck from each other, the friction of inadvertently beautiful or deliberately composed sounds, there was a quiet, cumulative force, like that of long lines of poetry wavering out from some central, spurring sense of sorrow and continually retreating to it, carrying it forward another line, seeing it through another stanza of incised lines, and another, and a wall of them. I wanted to read them more deeply, to crack the code. . . .

I said them to myself. Nearly everyone facing the wall was saying the names, often aloud, confiding them to someone near, sometimes laughing, struck by something peculiar in a name, or reciting a single line of names several times, because of the way certain names fitted together; other people told how many names they'd found of those they'd known—counting them up, pleased to have found them, the way you can be pleased at locating on an unfamiliar map some place you know exists. There was a queer catharsis in this finding, queer because it opened into another sort of yearning, or maybe a yearning that simply was, and, by the finding of a name and the fraction of an instant of recognition, the eye's delight in reading what it knew, was made clear as something that would endure, that could not be eased by the finding of a name so much as thrown into relief by it, exposed. There seemed to be an almost irresistible impulse, when one found a name, to touch it, to stroke the length of the inscription, to impress upon the reflective black something as slight as the ghostly humidity of one's handprint; to cover the name for a moment, to shield it, to make it private; to separate it for a moment from the locked vertical mass of the almost endless others. The number of the dead, in the mounting lines of inscriptions with rigid left-hand margin and ragged right-hand margin (this is reversed on the west wall: there the right-hand margin is the rigid one), was suddenly clear in a physical way, for you had to search among them, you had to pass by thousands of names to find one that meant something to you, and if you glanced away an instant you'd miss it, as surely as you'd miss a wedding ring on a beach; yet those names you passed by—skimmed in order to dismiss them or considered briefly for something out of the ordinary—worked on you as well, inflicting a steadily growing, almost subliminal pressure, which was your awareness of the uncannily great number and the irreducible singularity of the lives that had been lost. In the deep panels of

> polished black the readers were mirrored, their reflections facing them from the list of names, so that you could see yourself, in a sense, in among the dead. . . .
>
> Nothing, really, kept me from returning to the world—only my desire to stay inside the flanking black walls until I had understood them, understood something.[2]

The Vietnam Veterans Memorial marks neither victory nor defeat; it celebrates neither hero nor statesman. It fails to tell what is being summed up and commemorated. It firms up no relationship—not to Vietnam, not to America. Radically ambiguous, it deprives sculpture of its imputed essentials. Without pedestal it seems to have no specific place. Like Brancusi's "Endless Column," it is all pedestal, and thus invites its viewers to crack its governing code, work things out for themselves, create meaning. What is the critic to take note of other than one of that infinity of stories which it withholds? What can he articulate other than his own reactions?

Because it made concessions to the expectations of award committees, politicians, corporate boards, the military, and the public, Lin's memorial reveals its minimalism less starkly than the projects of artists who have rolled sawed redwood timber into a gallery, placed mirrors in the landscape, or sculptured wind and water. Hans Haacke, largely known for his kinetic sculpture, can be seen to have followed his own advice to "make something indeterminate that always looks different, the shape of which cannot be predicted precisely. . . . Make something that cannot 'perform' without the assistance of its environment. . . . Make something sensitive to light and temperature, that is subject to air currents. . . . Make something that lives in time and makes the 'spectator' experience time."[3] If art inheres not in structures such as Haake's (or Lin's) but in the transactions they engender, the structures succeed insofar

---

[2] Elizabeth Talent, *New Yorker,* March 18, 1985. Reprinted by permission; © 1985, The New Yorker Magazine, Inc.

[3] Quoted by Jack Burnham in Alan Sonfist, ed., *Art in the Land* (New York: E. P. Dutton, 1983), p. 113. See also Lucy R. Lippard, ed., *Six Years: The Dematerialization of the Art Object from 1966–1972* (New York: Praeger, 1973); and Rosalind Krauss, "Sculpture in the Expanded Field," in Hal Foster, ed., *The Anti-Aesthetic* (Port Townsend, Wash.: Bay Press, 1983); Gregory Battcock, ed., *Minimal Art: A Critical Anthology* (New York: Dutton, 1968); Nilos Stangos, ed., *Concepts of Modern Art* (New York: Harper & Row, 1974); Calvin Tomkins, *The Bride and the Bachelors* (New York: Viking, 1968).

as they "live in time"—that is, insofar as they keep inspiring transactions between the spectator's unexamined, objectified sense of time and what the spectator keeps making of the artist's presentations. They work to the extent that time as known, as meticulously clocked, is loosened and displaced, that time is deprived of its autonomy, its power to dominate and organize experience. In deconstructing, the artist provides a clearing which beckons others to come to new terms with the world.

The effort to clear an arena within which transactions take place is manifest in the various large-scale projects executed by Christo (he dropped his last name when he came to New York from Bulgaria in 1964). One of them, his "Running Fence" (1976), made the people of Valley Ford in California's Sonoma County remember the parties, crowds, and traffic jams, the record number of hamburgers sold, the network TV publicity—all the theatrical events sparked by the fluttering, shimmering expanse of white nylon anchored for some two weeks on cables and steel posts along a zigzagging twenty-four-mile stretch through the coastal zone north of San Francisco. "There were lots of people here," L. S. Brooks, manager of the Valley Ford branch of the Bank of America, remembered. "You couldn't park in town. They came early and stayed late. The three girls and I worked very hard during the last three weeks of construction and during the time it was up, but we enjoyed every minute of it. It was a happy time. It was great, great for the community."[4] To install his curtain, Christo had the help of contractors, engineering consultants, sixty-five skilled workers, and over three hundred college students. Beyond these collaborators—and beyond the local merchants—there had been attorneys to appeal the denial of a land-use permit; and beyond them, some sixty financial sponsors, art dealers, and collectors of Christo's sketches and collages; and beyond them, Jeanne-Claude, his wife who publicized the venture and raised the two million dollars needed to sustain it. Over a period of three years fifty-nine ranchers were persuaded (and paid) to give permission to let some 2,200 sheets of nylon, each eighteen feet high and sixty-eight feet wide, snake across their property toward the coast. What is more, Christo had overcome the resistance of all but one of the public agencies charged with safeguarding the environment. Vigorously oppor-

---

[4] Quoted by Jim Wood, "The 'Fantastic' Fence that Ran Away with Their Hearts," *San Francisco Examiner,* September 19, 1977, p. 1.

tunistic, he cajoled and conned his way toward success, coping with individual skepticism, local politics, bureaucratic routines, and an economy geared to appreciate palpable pay-offs. In the end, Christo acted outside the law; to extend his fence the last few miles into the waters of the Pacific, he defied the ruling of the California Coast Commission.

Today, the fence is gone. Only preliminary drawings, legal briefs, the record of some sixteen public hearings, cost estimates, travel vouchers, engineering reports, contracts, bills of lading, receipts of money spent, an elaborate environmental impact report, a documentary film of the fence's construction, and Sonoma County Landmark No. 24 (a solitary fence pole) remain as testimony to Christo's cunning and energy. Nothing but these artifacts, most of which were funneled into the art market, intimate what had actually spanned the countryside, what despite its sheer sweep and range had been devoid of message and point, generating only by-products, achieving only side-effects, ultimately amounting to nothing weighty enough to be regarded as rational. Yet Christo's ephemeral object had given shape to his own impulses, transformed a landscape, and activated a quiescent populace. It had been the occasion for relating hundreds, perhaps thousands, of previously unrelated people. It had dramatically linked whoever reacted to Christo's ambition—critics, ecologist, philistines, rival local artists (they constituted a Committee to Stop the Fence), journalists, viewers of TV news, teachers of courses in art appreciation (the fence has become the cover picture of a widely used text, Duane Preble's *Artforms*), and not least scholars talking about ways for relating entrepreneurial talent, art, and politics.

I HAVE BEEN calling attention to Christo's performance not only because it defines the ground for coming to terms with alien powers but also because its meagerness (as I see it from the distance in a documentary film) will not engage us deeply. To have staying power, a work art—any construction—must *keep* engaging alien powers at its margin. It must *keep* working under changing conditions. What matters is its capacity for *remaining* ambiguous, flexible, and light enough to change under changing circumstances and yet firm and grounded enough to keep making its presence felt.

Judged in these terms, performances are tests of the performer's ability to range widely and deeply enough to *stay* in motion. If he lands too close to the familiar, includes too little of the unmediated turbulence at the margin of his consciousness, his act—his very life—becomes stale and disappears; if he moves too far and includes too much, his act becomes unbearably mindboggling. To keep his balance, he must remain alert. If he tires he will move either toward the lightness of nonperformance (nothing will be there) or the heaviness of nonperformance (everything will be there). In either case he will move toward inaction and oblivion, for he will have lost his balance. Like Matisse, he must keep oscillating between heavy substance and light arabesque, stopping at neither one nor the other, merely celebrating his dance between them.

My metaphor of the balancing of heaviness and lightness is drawn from the story Milan Kundera relates in *The Unbearable Lightness of Being* (1984). Tomas, a middle-aged Prague surgeon at the novel's center, regards two women, Sabina and Tereza, as "the two poles of life, separated and irreconcilable, yet equally appealing." His relation to Sabina is light and casual. While he remains an incorrigible womanizer, he marries Tereza, who is passive, reliable, tradition-bound. Shortly after the Russians invade Czechoslovakia the married couple leaves Prague and settles in Geneva, where, as it happens, Sabina lives buoyantly in exile. After Tereza has decided she must return home, Tomas briefly delights in his freedom from commitments. But: "On Monday, he was hit by a weight the like of which he had never known. The tons of steel of the Russian tanks were nothing compared with it." He reunites with Tereza, with occupied Prague. Asked by the Party to choose between retracting insignificant political remarks in an article he had published or losing his job, his very profession as surgeon, he refuses to recant. Harassed by the police, forced to become a highrise window washer, he makes light of the heaviness of his new situation: he treats his job as a vacation, a lark, a chance to become a voyeur. Ultimately he and Tereza are driven to move to the country, to what remains of the crushing conventions of village life. At the same time Sabina continues to flout convention by rejecting all commitments. She easily moves from city to city, from Europe to the New World, where she dissolves in the amorphous lightness of America. It was only Tomas on his involuntary "vacation" who had experienced a moment of precarious poise. In occupied country on the smallest of stages, he had been free to play seriously. Framed by an oppressive regime, assigned to wash windows, he had integrated heaviness and lightness. His brief performance had related elements that annihilate us either by crushing us in particularity or dissolving us in ethereal realms.

A PERFORMANCE MAY feature anything whatever—the washing of a window, the preparing of a dinner, the designing of a political platform, or the teaching of a skill. Yet whatever it explicitly features it also demonstrates how nimbly the performer manages both to keep on the move and stay in touch with his or her material. It's touch and go, hit and run. He shows himself occupied by his subject matter and yet able to take it lightly—lightly enough to introduce new elements. From him we can learn to appreciate the discipline for making performances suspenseful, dramatic, and alive—simply interesting. We can note that like Socrates's dialogues they refer not only to the heavy subjects of justice or friendship but also to the way the subject is handled, to the ingenuity necessary to encourage increasingly elaborate reflections. They exhibit stratagems for staying in touch with the unrefined feelings of one's companions while remaining sufficiently disengaged to continue one's transactions. They give instruction in composition and composure—in keeping one's balance even while including progressively more phenomena in the effort to stay in touch, to keep talking, to relate.

Such a balance is lost whenever a performer moves *fully* into the material featured by the performance. Thus an actor properly keeps himself from rendering more than the surface manifestation of his emotions. He is preoccupied by his appearance. He knows that he betrays himself and his community, as Plato warned, when his act unleashes passions which, to maintain consciousness, he must hold in check. Knowing how readily people become victims of their passions, he keeps himself (and his audience) conscious of his performance as performance. He makes it transparent that he is but acting. He *acts* the murderous queen without becoming one. He *recites* his lines, *gives* his speech, *expresses* his rage, love, chagrin, or grief. Thus his murderous behavior or his cry of remorse must be seen as enacted: it's not the real thing. His acts invariably relate to a world larger than any particular reality which, to the extent that it becomes exclusive, would grab and absorb him. The closer he comes to being absorbed by the particular demands of his role, the more he must watch himself. And as he tires out, he will reduce the richness of the unenacted dimension of his act: he narrows its range and finally flees from the intensity of the limelight.

When he fails to balance attachment and detachment, his act—his play—will come to a dead end. It will be for real. As his energy flags or his patience wears out, as he loses what is aptly called his temper, he succumbs to the forces impinging on his consciousness—ultimately making them indubitably present. Unable to come to terms with them, he will be in their grip. He then is as driven as Melville's Captain Ahab who, deeply injured by a whale, could not help but define his injury as dead real and so treats the whale as unredeemable. Regarding himself as mere invalid, Ahab fails as artist: he eliminates the whale to reestablish his validity, to recover his balance. His encounter with an all-too-real whale—a veritable killer—had exhausted his resources for upholding that view of health and wholeness which consecrates pain and pleasure indiscriminately, which assumes that the very ritual of consecrating is healing, which simply knows of no *real* injury, no *real* pain, no *real* invalid. Seeking to recover, Ahab was carried away by what Melville called his "narrow-flowing monomania." Attached to a notion of health that excludes the pain he had suffered, he proceeded to do Justice whatever the cost to himself and his crew. He was no Nietzschean saint beyond good and evil for whom the love of the particular is informed by the love of the whole, for whom all parts are suffused by their opposites.

When driven off-stage and put out of action, when fully acted upon and merely reacting, we cannot help but lose our distance, our humanity. Only in action can we appear as acting slaves or acting masters. It is in action alone that neither success nor failure, neither life nor death are real. Only when bringing our various parts into relationship do we know that everything entails its opposite. Only then do we know that nothing *is*—nothing except a process of action which cannot *be,* cannot be incarnate, without ceasing to be.

Of course there is no way to conceptualize the shuttling between Being and Process. Concepts are designed, after all, to *stop* the flow between our so-called parts. Concepts *work* insofar as they freeze and polarize, and therefore particularize and distinguish. They *make* things distinguished. They are quite simply judgments which disclose where we want to draw the line, where we desire to end. We employ them as we employ punchlines—to arrest further thought, analysis, interpretation, fantasy. We need them because they bring the unbearable flow to an end. We need them even when, still duplicitous, we also aim to survive like Ishmael, like Melville himself—seeking to survive the sinking of the *Pequod* and to surface as a buoyant orphan conscious in an endless flow of forces.

TO SURVIVE AND remain at play is to be engaged in the continuous experimental process of testing and changing the rules so as to extend the range of controlled experience. Extending consciousness entails a readiness to enact rules for including underprivileged elements within our play, rules that *legitimate* impulses identified as infantile or decadent or perverse. It entails a readiness to review—and thus make present—the lines drawn between actor and spectator, parent and child, teacher and student, doctor and patient. To move toward making everything present is to keep the distinctions between past and the future as much in suspense as the distinction between inside and outside. It is to support an ecological politics, one that makes us mindful both of the infinite range of our interests and of our capacity for orchestrating all that comes and goes.

It is only in such an open-ended politics that we can learn which specific checks and balances keep us from ending, what kind of past to invent or repress so as to enrich the present. When oriented by nothing but the situations in which we find ourselves we can appreciate the risks taken by Agnellus, the ninth-century bishop of Ravenna, who wrote the biographies of his predecessors with scrupulous disregard for lifeless facts:

> Where I have not found any history of any of these bishops, and have not been able by conversation with aged men, or inspection of the monuments, or from any other authentic source, to obtain information concerning them, in such a case, in order that there might not be a break in the series, I have *composed* the life myself, with the help of God and the prayers of the brethen.[5]

IN SONOMA COUNTY in the late 1970s, Christo had kept his balance in the midst of the turbulence he generated. In retrospect it is easy to note, I

---

[5] Quoted in Herbert J. Muller, *The Uses of the Past* (New York: Oxford University Press, 1952), p. 237, emphasis supplied.

think, that Christo did well—did well enough. Had he imposed less than his nylon curtain (a powdered line along back roads?) he might have been ignored. More (the Berlin Wall?) might have led to an injunction. True, the curtain was but a tactful trespass, a noninsistent crossing of property lines. Yet however brief its presence, it did respond to the quite human desire for some sort of completion: something specific was quite patently there. "The Fence," one Valley Ford resident is reported to have said, "gave you a reason for looking."[6] Christo had cause to assume that in Sonoma County of the 1970s reasons—palpable pretexts—were needed even though his minimalist aesthetics dictated no specific pretext as proper. Maneuvering between a weighty monument and an unnamable spirit, he settled for neither. It is useful to recall and appreciate how close he played it.

In an account of the fence's construction, Calvin Tomkins reported that "everything that had to do with it—television and film crews, legal action by people who violently opposed the project, even a slightly startled herd of cows—inevitably became part of his aesthetic process."[7] Writing in the *Co-Evolution Quarterly,* Peter Warshall noted that Christo "brought together postmasters and aerodynamic engineers, botanists and sheep ranchers, lawyers, art museum directors, and rancher's wives." More than that, people saw themselves from the point of view of others: "roles were reversed."[8] Christo's intervention had changed the grid that convention imposes on life; he had shifted the cultural overlay that organizes how people perceive themselves and one another. Insofar as those who tried to stop Christo's project emerged as participants, he had recognized, included, and enlarged submerged aspects of reality. He had created a playground—a stage, a political forum—which integrated whatever emerged—wind, people, resentments, hostilities. In Tomkins's words, he used everything:

---

[6] Jim Wood, "The 'Fantastic' Fence."

[7] Calvin Tomkins, "Running Fence," *New Yorker,* March 28, 1977, p. 43. See also Werner Spies, *The Running Fence Project* (New York: Abrams, 1978), and the documentary film, "Running Fence" (1978).

[8] Peter Warshall, "Christo's Running Fence," *Co-Evolution Quarterly,* Winter 1976/1977, pp. 70–73.

> Ultimately, Christo accepted the wrath of the McChesneys, of the Raymonds, of Bill Kortum and the rest as part of the process—not only accepted it but used it, just as he used the landscape and the ocean and the weather, the legal and political ramifications, the practical efficiency of his engineers, the sometimes scattered energy of the young workers, and the chaotic and unrelenting intrusion of the photographers and filmmakers and journalists on hand to record the event. Using everything is his stock in trade.[9]

Whatever his qualms, he proceeded in violation of coastal regulations so as to stretch the last piece of the fence to a raft in the Pacific. "I completely work within the American system by being illegal, like everyone else—if there is no illegal part, the project is less reflective of the system." He claimed that he had not acted as some sort of conartist inserting some sort of unreal make-belief into the landscape: "Some people say I make theater art, but it is not theater, because there is not one element of make-believe anywhere."[10] Yet surely the claim is disingenuous, for he did make people believe in the fence. Moreover, he made this belief credible by treating whatever he encountered, including the landscape itself, as obstinate realities that had to be accommodated and paid off in political transactions. Yet if he succeeded in restructuring reality, he was scarcely guided by some abstract notion of beauty. Instead, he acted pragmatically in the light of his quite practical view of the limits of his power in a specific historical and social situation. Providing a pretext for inducing ignored aspects of reality to make their public appearance, he put what was believed to be reality to the test. To say it emphatically, *he staged a public demonstrations—an experiment verifying the conditions under which reality becomes a living process.*

But it needs to be added that while Christo's projects make human environments more luminous, they ultimately betray no impulse to change it. They merely—merely!—lead him and others to *see*. His performances are free from that impulse to incarnate a transcendent reality which inspires modernist work such as Barnett Newman's paintings of "Stations

---

[9] Tomkins, "Running Fence," p. 80.

[10] Ibid.

of the Cross." Nor do they give expression to that hope for the future evident in the Constructivist movement in Russia, in Mondrian's positive response to the city, or above all in the Bauhaus school's sublimation of technology. Christo's enterprises slide into that postmodernism which, holding out no hope, merely intensifies the elements of a world caught up in an ungovernable, self-enacting process.

ROBERT IRWIN'S CAREER no less than Christo's expresses the struggle to structure the world and yet to let it be. Again and again, Irwin desired to eliminate the frames and outlines of his constructions, desiring only to paint, not to paint anything, not to produce anything, *only to paint.* Since his art kept veering toward nonexistence, it is fortunate that Irwin should have found a listener in Lawrence Weschler, who encouraged Irwin to keep talking while making a record of his maneuvers. In the 1960s, in Weschler's unobtrusive account. Irwin

> produced ten canvases, each with two straight lines hand-splayed over a monotone ground, into which they virtually disappeared. Although the lines' placement had been painstakingly calibrated for the most neutral effect, each canvas still read as "a painting of two lines," and Irwin next wondered, "Is it possible to paint a painting without subject and without linear mark?" The result, between 1964 and 1966, was a series of ten large, slightly bowed, white canvases overspread with a fine peppering of tiny dots in two opposing colors. The dots seemed to cancel each other out, halating around the edges; the paintings vibrated with an uncanny energy. But although these paintings had successfully resolved the question they had addressed, Irwin felt they were compromised by the frame itself, the rectangle that arbitrarily bound them in and likewise bound out the varied world of phenomena around them.
>
> He then wondered if it were possible to paint a painting without a frame. The resultant investigations produced a series of remarkable disc paintings (1966–67). A convex white disc was thrust out about two feet from the wall, hovering, and when Irwin played floodlights on it from each of the four corners, projecting a four leaf clover of shadows onto the white wall behind, it was extremely difficult to fathom where the gray-white disks left off and the mothy shadows began. The shield itself read alternately as flat, bulging, or collapsed, and even from virtual profile the truth was

> elusive. The entire space seemed to float. While these discs had effectively eliminated the frame from the art object, they did ask the viewer to focus; they still required an attitude of focus; they still demanded of the viewer a heightened level of attention aimed at one area of the room.[11]

By 1968 Irwin realized, as he told Weschler, that "it had been a long journey. Starting out from my more or less naive approach as a painter, I had now arrived at a point where, in a sense, I had dismantled the whole thing: image, line, frame, focus, transcendability. I'd been dismantling the art endeavor, but in the process I'd dismantled myself." He said, "I cut the knot. I got rid of the studio, sold all the things I owned, all the equipment, all my stuff; and without knowing what I was going to do with myself or how I was going to spend my time, I simply stopped being an artist. . . . I just quit." But not for long. Having come to a dead end, Irwin still welcomed interviews, still did not dispense with language and metaphor. He realized he would still "have to drive a car, listen to the news, buy a Coke." Irwin's art dealer maintained that Irwin "simply refused to play by the art world's rules—to politic for commissions, to attend to documentation, and so forth—and so he's become invisible." Yet the fact is that Irwin remained visible enough designing projects, supervising museum installations of his work, writing catalog introductions, above all conceptualizing, talking, lecturing.

Striving to apprehend the world without mediating symbols, he was engaged in the impossible venture of conveying nothing and yet communicating, of sensualizing space without imposing on it. He sought to turn his awareness of the inexpressible *presence* of places and situations into art. He wanted paintings without images, without anything memorable. He wanted viewers simply to view, to dispense with mediation and comparison. His work had to be absent—light beyond documentation. But how? Seeking passivity, he decided to be merely ready, as he said, "to go anywhere, anytime for anybody, for anything. I made myself very available—and I made myself available for free." He toured colleges, talked, and produced a welter of constructions designed to enhance the experi-

---

[11] Lawrence Weschler, *Seeing is Forgetting the Thing One Sees: A Life of Contemporary Artist Robert Irwin* (Berkeley and Los Angeles: University of California Press, 1982), pp. 87, 91, 155–56, 163, 174, 189.

ences of whoever moved through them. Yet the negative thrust of his performances, he realized, inescapably contradicted his desire to communicate. There was no evading the conventions of the art world even if only to show their failure to present the emptiness of his work. He wanted nothing more consequential than to invite others simply to apprehend the world. No doubt, he hoped this would *make* no one apprehensive or drive anyone to reimpose structures that might once again discriminate against the plenitude of Being. In 1975 he transformed an area of Chicago's Museum of Contemporary Art by laying a black tape in such a way that several people who had been working at the museum for years were surprised and asked him whether he had added the room's central post—a post that had been actually in the room all along. "Now what I did had a minimal physical or intellectual being, no literate meanings, no symbolic references, and no art world contents; and yet you were clearly conscious of a presence. When you turned around to walk out of the space, you suddenly became aware of the post." He had made viewers aware of overlooked, unmentioned aspects of experience. Noting that a black tape of no significance nevertheless had an effect, Irwin concluded that art requires no explicit activity of any kind. Yet as he expanded his operations, he observed that considerably more than a strip of tape was required to organize the perceptions of others outside the walls of museums. Accordingly, he carefully spread paint over a square outlined by crosswalks of New York City's Fifth Avenue and 42nd Street. Whatever the scale of this performance, he still sought only to call attention to what had been unremarkable—not previously remarked on. More than that, he wished not only to eliminate the work of art but also his own presence in his creative act. Departing from work that, in his terms, is site dominant, site adjusted, and site specific, he moved, as he wrote in 1985, toward installations he called "site conditioned/determined"—where "the sculptural response draws all its cues (reasons for being) from its surrounding." What he demanded of himself was "an intimate, hands-on reading of the site" as condition for sheer responsiveness.[12]

Unavoidably, it all remained an exasperating, impossible enterprise. Irwin could not accept his sublime invisibility—the imperceivable, un-

---

[12] Robert Irwin, *Being and Circumstance: Notes toward a Conditional Art* (San Francisco: Lapis Press, 1985), p. 27.

marketable dimension of his activities. Because there was no avoiding working toward a fixed end-product *and* withdrawing from it, he finally showed himself as neither creator nor destroyer of definitive forms. His scrupulous duplicity, his endless shifting, was to be sustained by his intense concern for the spaces he encountered, his reverence for whatever promised continuous possibilities for perceptual acts. Irwin cared groundlessly, gratuitously.

As an effort to move toward increasing awareness of phenomena which elude us when we focus and pay attention, Irwin's journey repeated Claude Monet's. Throughout his life, Monet had struggled to depict only "what I see." He began with landscapes that *he* had landscaped—that is, specifically designed to lend themselves to being painted. Later he composed, as Roger Shattuck has written in a compelling essay, "the fluid vibratory substance that he seemed to see." He painted "matter so thoroughly penetrated by his eye as to appear as a field, as lines of force dissolved into energy." And finally "he was almost *hearing* the landscape. . . . He listened to the field, where figure and ground tend to fuse and only vibration remains." Shattuck says that "our experience of focusing, noticing, and paying attention conspires to make this unprocessed 'first' impression inaccessible" and that accordingly Monet sought to make the surfaces of his canvases increasingly fluid and elusive. "In Monet's very last paintings the world of appearances—both the still recognizable garden motifs and the nonfigurative traces of his gesturing brush—has metamorphized from the transitory into permanence. . . . The world is in constant flux, yes, not on its surface but behind, in its depths."[13]

IT IS ABOVE all a disciplined evasion of every fixed substance that is the ground shared by the various artists I have been singling out. Oppressed by the weight of modernity, theirs is the posture of the psychoanalyst who persists in remaining in a state of readiness, of availability, a state in which he or she takes pains to keep from expecting either this or that of the patient. Such work combines, as Anton Ehrenzweig has noted, attentiveness to the particular and indifference to its value: "The artist's vacant,

---

[13] Roger Shattuck, *The Innocent Eye: On Modern Literature and the Arts* (New York: Farrar, Straus & Giroux, 1984), pp. 231, 239, 235, 239.

unfocused stare pays attention to the smallest detail however far removed from the consciously perceived figure. The uncompromising democracy which refuses to make any distinction between the significance of the elements building the work of art belongs to the essence of artistic rigour."[14] This active-passive posture sustains the unfocused seeing Robert Venturi has encouraged as teacher of architecture by asking his students to suspend judgment while scanning the artifacts littering America's urbanized landscape. Venturi's own designs work to redeem the strangeness he sees when he fails to focus. For the 1976 United States Bicentennial, Venturi organized the Smithsonian Institution's "Signs of Life: Symbols in the American City," an exhibit of unretouched signs, billboards, and furnished interiors of three American houses as well as the constructions lining a fictitious "Route 66." Making the most of suburban sprawl, embracing it uncritically, he exhibited not its beauty, merely its vitality.[15]

Welcoming the flux at the margin of his life and yet letting them be, the artist remains in a position of intense expectancy. Though intent on seeing what happens, he isn't looking for anything in particular. Ready for whatever may occur, he treats nothing as a failure, exception, digression, accident, or distortion. He knows situations in terms *they* provide—not as he wills them to be. His novels, paintings, dances, poems, earthworks, sculptures, or plays embrace elements of life that he has come across, that have crossed his path without making him cross.

Declining to impose, the artist displays a state of being for which we have no single concept, to which we can scarcely give clear thought, to which we can grant no status in our rationally organized mental life. His way of allowing things to become increasingly alive, his *making* endless allowances, is an affirmative effort to be resigned, to let things be. Our very language keeps us from integrating such active passivity, such passive activity. We cannot formulate an aesthetics that endorses producing non-products or creating sounds of silence. We cannot communicate the mean-

---

[14] Anton Ehrenzweig, *The Hidden Order of Art: A Study in the Psychology of Artistic Imagination* (Berkeley and Los Angeles: University of California Press, 1967), pp. 23, 29–30.

[15] Robert Venturi, Denise Scott Brown, and Steven Izenour, *Learning from Las Vegas* (Cambridge,: M.I.T. Press, 1972); Renwick Gallery, *Signs and Symbols* (Washington, D.C.: National Collection of Fine Arts, Smithsonian Institution, 1976).

ing of passive resistance, of vehemently *doing* nothing. What can we conceivably mean when we say we're hopeful, but aren't hoping for anything? A prospective mother who says she's expecting but has no particular expectations sounds queer, especially were she to add that she is expecting pure potentiality. Nor would she be more convincing were she to explain that while she will impose no specific ideal of the Good Child, she will nevertheless be intensively active—actively encouraging everything to *be*. Yet this incongruous commitment to inclusiveness is precisely that of the artist whose projects unite assertive and nonassertive qualities—however hard it is to see this when these qualities are kept separate by being ascribed on the one hand to men and on the other to women.[16]

Looking at the arts of modernism, we tend to see only broken plots, shattered language, decomposed music, randomly mixed legacies—the whole a mere wasteland. We can hardly allow that nothing but man-made forms relate and thereby unify what we conventionally polarize. We want to assume that when Melville has Billy Budd relate elements of experience that have lost all meaning, Melville still appeals to a reality behind the world of meaningless appearances. Yet no authoritatively given order of things reconciles the dreadfully loose ends of his story. On board a God-forsaken ship of war Billy can do no more at the end than ask an absent God to bless Captain Vere. Neither he nor the captain who has ordered Billy's execution speaks with God-given authority: nothing whatever transcends the inexorable Articles of War. *Both* the executioner and the executed are at the end locked like Melville into a system of unlimited state power—a system Billy Budd nonetheless acts to affirm.[17]

---

[16] "The contradiction between acting (demonstration) and experience (empathy) often leads the uninitiated to suppose that only one or the other can be manifest in the work of the actor. . . . In reality it is a matter of two mutually hostile processes which fuse in the actor's work; his performance is not just composed of a bit of the one and a bit of the other." Bertolt Brecht, "A Short Organum for the Theatre," *Accent* 2 (Winter 1951): 179–205.

[17] This is my deviant reading of *Billy Budd* after pondering Michael Paul Rogin's *Subversive Genealogy: The Politics and Art of Herman Melville* (New York: Knopf, 1983), chap. 9. Rogin interprets Melville's work by relating it to Melville's family and kin and, more comprehensively, to an emerging America increasingly absorbed by the power relations implicit in individualism, capitalist acquisition, and impersonal industrialism. Rogin takes no stand independent of his text: like Melville, he appears impotent at the end of genealogy—and yet gives voice to his fate.

3 STRATEGIES FOR DETACHMENT

FOR postmodernists, appeals to a fixed order of natural rights or transcultural values ring hollow. Their performances are not fortified by the hopefulness of Yeats, Eliot, Pound, Hamsun, Lawrence, and Mann, modernists who could still assume the existence of some wholesome reality beyond the process of modernization, some stable transhistorical ground on which to take one's stand. Elaborately circular, the language of postmodernism assumes no definitive points of arrival or departure; it seizes nothing decisively. In the end, postmodernists are in possession of nothing but their sheer consciousness—that disembodied, ungrounded awareness which Camus attributed to Sisyphus, who cherished his impotent self while serenely enduring his fate—the punishment of the gods. Dismantling every intimation of focused potency, postmodernists will not allow anything to *be*. Unblinking voyeurs within the culture of utilitarian calculations, their strategy is to distance themselves from it by practicing a politics which is so demanding that it is easy to doubt the possibility of extending it.

Resolved to come to terms with the prevailing finalities without embracing any of their own, postmodernists value the kind of detachment which finds expression in the choreographed complications of Merce Cunningham, the alienating devices employed by Bertolt Brecht, the intricate excesses of deconstructionists in literature, the black comedy of performance art, the graffiti imposed on the numbing undulation of subway cars. They invest in diversions. Fearful of ending, they are the least definitive of human beings—picaresque nomads who, forever learning how not to die, design detours and relish digressions. Feeling bound by neither the promises they make nor the beliefs they profess, they keep looking at the world crookedly so as to see more of it. Lengthening the time between departures and arrivals whether in business or domestic life, sex or sport, they evade the deadly rapture of success. Mountain climbers who disdain ropes, they put obstacles in the way of reaching the top or coming to the point.[1] They miss deadlines and keep struggling against the conviction that God or Nature has determined their schedules. For them births and deaths are not traumas inflicted but dramas enacted. They see all fixed objectives as merely man-made points of reference. Redefining the openings and closings, deciding on their own entries and exits, they seek to keep the curtain up and perform on Dionysian ground beyond which—the vision is that of Nietzsche—there is but an expanse of pure vitality,

---

[1] "Mountaineers often work under numerous self-imposed handicaps. Equipment is restricted to a Spartan minimum. Mechanized transport is forgone in favor of walking. Help from others in the form of porters, Sherpas, or guides is reserved for the extremes of expeditions or for those with only limited skill, such as tourists in the Alps. Some go so far in the search for balance that they may at times even restrict the effectiveness of their own bodies by an avoidance of conditioning programs and by almost enthusiastic acceptance of heavy drinking. Those who climb less technical peaks limit the time they allow themselves to reach the summits, rushing from one top to another on a busy peak-bagging weekend. Technical hardware is employed, when necessary, with caution and restraint; fixed ropes are kept to a minimum and used only in a prescribed fashion." (Richard G. Mitchell, Jr., *Mountain Experience* [Chicago: University of Chicago Press, 1963]), p. 76.) The practices of deconstructionism are analogous. Textual analysis, Stanley Fish contends, should never come to the point, or at least "no sooner than the pressure to do so becomes unbearable (psychologically). Coming to the point is the goal of a criticism that believes in content, in extractable meaning, in the utterance of a repository. Coming to the point fulfills a need that most literature deliberately frustrates . . . , the need to simplify and close." (Stanley Fish, *Is There a Text in the Class?* [Cambridge: Harvard University Press, 1980], p. 52.)

> a monster of energy, without beginning, without end; a firm, iron magnitude of force that does not grow bigger or smaller, that does not expend itself but only transforms itself; as a whole, of unalterable size, a household without expenses or losses, but likewise without increase or income; enclosed by "nothingness" as by a boundary; not something blurry or wasted, not something endlessly extended, but set in a definite space as a definite force, and not a space that might be "empty" here or there, but rather as force throughout, as a play of forces and waves of forces, at the same time one and many, increasing here and at the same time decreasing there; a sea of forces flowing and rushing together, eternally changing, eternally flooding back, with tremendous years of recurrence, with an ebb and a flood of its forms; out of the simplest forms striving toward the most complex, out of stillest, most rigid, coldest forms toward the hottest, most turbulent, most selfcontradictory, and then again returning home to the simple out of this abundance, out of the play of contradictions back to the joy of concord, still affirming itself in this uniformity of its courses and its years blessing itself as that which must return eternally, as a becoming that knows no satiety, no disgust, no weariness: this, my *Dionysian* world of the eternally self-creating, the eternallly self-destroying, this mystery world of the two-fold voluptuous delight, my "beyond good and evil," without goal, unless the joy of the circle is itself a goal; without will, unless a ring feels good will toward itself—do you want a *name* for this world? A *solution* for all its riddles? A *light* for you, too, you best-concealed, strongest, most intrepid, most midnightly men? *This world is the will to power—and nothing besides!* And you yourselves are also this will to power—and nothing besides.[2]

"*And nothing besides*." Nietzsche intoned in opposition to that longing for limiting human activities by grounding them in God's unchanging intentions.

WHETHER AS MODERNIST or as postmodernist, the artist's "play of forces" are far from freefloating. His (or her) projects accept the most

---

[2] Friedrich Nietzsche, *The Will to Power,* trans. Walter Kaufmann (New York: Vantage, 1967), p. 549.

familiar of realities, however lightly he treats them. Although Whistler titled his painting "Arrangement in Grey and Black No. 1," he made his mother its specific subject. Monet's water lilies, Irwin's black tape, Christo's valley curtain, and Venturi's "Route 66" are all quite manifestly present. More or less emphatically, they occupy some discrete place during some specific time. In need of pretexts, in need of some quite specific subject matter so as to remain in the company of others—indeed, to remain at home in the world—the artist will compromise and postpone that kind of exhaustive seeing which, as Valery said, consists of forgetting the names of the things one sees. The works of such an artist will inevitably fall short of the nameless all-comprehensiveness that absorbs the mystic. They are the products of social experiments limited by contexts defined pragmatically by all-too-exhaustible human beings.

Communal transactions, such experiments acknowledge our need for dependable, familiar concepts—for shelters without which we cannot come to terms with Otherness. I am but assenting to William James's argument:

> The substitution of concepts and their connections, of a whole conceptual order, in short, for the immediate perceptual flow, thus widens enormously our mental panorama. Had we no concepts we should live simply by "getting" each successive moment of experience, as the sessile sea-anemone on its rock receives whatever nourishment the wash of the waves may bring. With concepts we go in quest of the absent, meet the remote, actively turn this way or that, bend our experience, and make it tell us whither it is bound. We change its order, run it backwards, bring far bits together and separate near bits, jump about over its surface instead of ploughing through its continuity, string its items on as many ideal diagrams as our mind can frame. All these are ways of *handling* the perceptual flux and *meeting* distant parts of it; and as far as this primary function of conception goes, we can only conclude it to be what I began by calling it, a faculty superadded to our barely perceptual consciousness for its use in practically adapting us to a larger environment than that of which brutes take account. We *harness* perceptual reality in concepts in order to drive it better to our ends.[3]

---

[3] William James, *Some Problems of Philosophy* (New York: Longmans, 1940), p. 51.

Conceptual systems enable us to pull ourselves together so that we might strike out anew. We require timetables and shopping lists, if only to outwit them. Again and again we need to believe that we are really young, really old, really passing through fixed stages of development, really moving across undeniable boundaries. We need curtains to be drawn, museums to have opening and closing hours. When life is felt to be interminable we need to tell ourselves that the *process* of art, like that of education, science, and politics, has a point. Drawn into wholly inconsequential processes, invited to settle for nothing but a state of irresolution, we are disconcerted and manage to recover only by identifying events, turning points, deadlines. The causes we ascribe to success or failure allow us to settle accounts, to identify bottom lines, to reach the top. If we didn't finalize, nothing would ever *be* a book, a career, a life. It wouldn't add up. Actors forever in transit, we'd have but empty scrapbooks to show for our performances. Seeking discrete terminal points, we settle for Death as if it were an event not of our own making.

To treat *every* structure as subject to change is surely to lose your balance, or at least to have others regard you as unbalanced. You become an actor like Christ, a danger to society. For you nothing specific remains of ultimate import. As you stay detached from a trapped animal, a drowning child, or a suffering community, you are perceived as *indecently* detached. Some specific response to the course of events is so *natural,* you will be reminded, that it is perverse to keep one's distance. Real tears are called for. Surely it was wrong (as J. D. Salinger's Buddy Glass wrote in his diary) that Abraham Lincoln had been so detached—so eloquent—at Gettysburg: pure rage, nothing reflective or even political, was called for by the bloodied ground on which Lincoln stood.

Only a god who embraces all Being has earned the right to distance himself from the ground the rest of us stand on. He alone is allowed to transcend the distinction between life and art, between weighty substance and insubstantial contrivances, between reality and appearance. Of him alone can it be said that beauty is in the eye of the beholder; he alone may see a mass execution as a dance, a bomb exploding in a crowd as the flowering of a rose. For mere human beings some events so clearly cry out for intervention that it becomes inhuman to keep one's distance, to see the loss of one's possessions as comic, torture as rhapsody, a holocaust as drama. We are made uneasy by the studied elegance of Diane Arbus's photographs of people who have relaxed in a state of deformity: their condition shouldn't be quite so impeccably depicted by so detached a photographer. Whether or not we are thrown off balance by Robert Altman's *M*A*S*H* or Stanley Kubrick's *Dr. Strangelove,* some humor, surely, is sick. Arbus and Altman and Kubrick may be whirling to excess.

Aware of our fear of losing our balance, the artist frames his experiments and treats the frames as real. Limiting his playfulness, he balances his detachment from structures with his concern for them. If in his *Day for Night* Truffaut acts the part of a film director who remains detached from the films he directs, he no less directs it. He brings it into focus, moves it toward culmination. Out of an understanding of how much knowledge his actors can bear he guards the boundary around his set: at critical moments he keeps his company from learning that bankers are threatening to cancel the movie and that one of their fellow players has just been killed in a highway crash. He withholds part of what he knows because his overriding concern is to make their common show go on, to keep relating as extravagantly as they can manage. And yet Truffaut shows himself to be limited like everyone else: his dreams reveal that he, too, needs contrivances—images of past films—for going on.

The structure that Truffaut treats as real is the rock climber's wall. Its immediacy goads him to complicate his life, to add to his relationships. Having scaled a formidable mountain, Kurt Diemberger has recalled the diverse feelings his climb successfully integrated:

> Then followed the dream of a rock-climb, vertical, overhanging, pitonless, with innumerable small holes and wrinkles—perfect free-climbing on a sheer wall, with an infinity of air around us. At such moments you are gloriously conscious of your fingers, your muscles; of the toes of your boots winning a hold on the rough Brenta rock; of the wall, close to your face, shining black, brown, and bright ochre amid the grey—like flower patterns in a carpet—and all of it high above the comb down there at the foot of the climb. You are enmeshed in a bright web of thoughts, on which you climb ever higher, pulling yourself upwards from hand-hold to hand-hold, foot-

> hold to foot-hold, towards an ever-increasing freedom, while everything below you falls away as you exalt yourself all the time.
>
> Down there at the bottom, you see the shadows of the towers lengthen, and feel that you belong to your mountain with every fibre of your being and yet, at the same time, here, high above the abyss, utterly free of mind and spirit, you are acutely aware that you have arms and legs—and a body to waft you upwards.[4]

Basketball players are no different from mountain climbers in respecting the obstinacy of the given. But even as they accept the demands of their court, they move toward a peak which Bill Russell remembers:

> The feeling would spread to the other guys, and we'd all levitate. Then the game would just take off, and there'd be a natural ebb and flow that reminded you of how rhythmic and musical basketball is supposed to be. I'd find myself thinking, "This is it. I want this to keep going," and I'd actually be rooting for the other team. When their players made spectacular moves, I wanted their shots to go into the bucket; that's how pumped up I'd be. I'd be out there talking to the other Celtics, encouraging them and pushing myself harder, but at the same time part of me would be pulling for the other players too.[5]

Whatever our need to keep our eyes on the ball—its obdurate reality—we no less need to distance ourselves.

"When a chess player looks at the board," Arthur Koestler has noted, "he does not see a static mosaic, a 'still life,' but a magnetic field of forces, charged with energy—as Faraday saw the stresses surrounding magnets and currents as curves in space; or as Van Gogh saw vortices in the skies of Provence."[6] Unable to see relationships, we are afflicted like the victims of prosopagnosia, who as a consequence of a brain lesion cannot recognize a face as a field of interrelated elements, who, in Oliver Sacks's words, "have to employ an elaborate, absurd, and indirect route,

---

[4] Kurt Diemberger, *Summits and Secrets* (London: George Allen and Unwin, 1971), p. 67.

[5] Bill Russell and Taylor Branch, *Second Wind* (New York: Ballantine Books, 1979), pp. 176–77.

[6] Quoted in David Spanier, *Total Chess* (New York: E. P. Dutton, 1984), p. 203.

involving a bit-by-bit analysis of meaningless and separate features."[7] Unable to detach ourselves, we are efficient computers, but fail to see.

THE DIFFICULTY OF remaining detached is strikingly evident in dance. Dance in particular tends to whirl performers out of their performance into that state of unreflective being which resolves the tensions that inspire it. The eroticism at the heart of dance tests one's ability to live with frustration—to block completion and remain unreconciled. Among contemporary dancers Merce Cunningham in particular has been devoted to providing obstacles designed to become the more formidable the closer the dancers move to the edge of consciousness. He expected, he said, "a complete awareness of the world and at the same time a detachment from it." Thus his choreography, unlike Martha Graham's, aims at maintaining the tension between brute experience and self-awareness—that is, with *maintaining* the arena for play. In an essay dealing with Cunningham's concerns, Roger Copeland has taken account of the multitude of his distancing devices—the toss of a coin for determining the arrangement of sequences, the sharp reversals of bodily movement, the incongruous separation of music and dance, the sudden disruption of themes which threaten to coalesce, the use of props and lighting to contradict expected audience perceptions.[8] His choreography complicates, dislocates, and interrupts. It opposes the impulse to do what comes naturally, to respond to the primal forces which music touches most intimately. Unlike Martha Graham, Cunningham deflects the drive for completion. Playing it cool, he demands an ironic, austere posture by letting only the most fleeting images unify fragments that are to remain distinct. His effects are summed up by Roger Copeland:

> The on-stage activity does not respect the traditional hierarchies of organization according to which dancers located downstage center automatically command our attention in a way that the dancers upstage left or right do

---

[7] See Oliver Sacks, "The Man Who Mistook His Wife for a Hat," *London Review of Books*, May 10–June 1, 1983.

[8] Roger Copeland, "The Politics of Perception," *Contact Quarterly* 6 (Winter, 1981): 16–23. Copeland contrasts Antonin Artaud's involvement and Bertolt Brecht's detachment in "Brecht, Artaud and the Hole in the Paper Sky," *Theatre* 9 (Summer 1978): 42–49.

> not. Cunningham refuses to tell us what to look at or listen to. We may decide to "background" or "turn off" a sound so as to focus more intently on the movement. (Perhaps it's significant that Mark Lancaster's setting for . . . "Tango" is a television set broadcasting a live picture, but with the sound turned off.) Or we may cultivate a skill John Cage calls "polyattentiveness"—the simultaneous apprehension of two or more unrelated phenomena. . . .
>
> Cunningham's work may not *symbolize* anything; but it does serve an end beyond itself: that of *perpetual training*. The importance of Cunningham's work ties not only in what we're given to see and hear, but in the way we see and hear what we're given.[9]

Cunningham's discipline is manifest in Bertolt Brecht's effort to break the hold of those ritualistically induced states of trance to which he believed his bourgeois audiences had succumbed: "The illusion created by the theater must be a partial one in order that it may always be recognized as an illusion. Reality . . . has to be altered by being turned into art, so that it can be seen to be alterable and treated as such. And this is why we too are inquiring into naturalness: we want to alter the nature of our social life."[10] His plays, Brecht kept saying, are nothing but plays, a bag of tricks, a set of props and illusions. They're unreal constructions, like the world outside. By tearing the smooth fabric of his narrative with inserted newsreels, Brecht counteracts the seductive quality of routines. He heightens awareness precisely as Christo does in a print which shows the Whitney Museum fastidiously wrapped, the wrapping calling attention to a building so familiar that passersby don't see it. A daily routine is broken. We are distanced—cast in the role of stranger, or, as in one of Chantal Ackerman's films, allowed to scan only the frozen surfaces of mundane life. Such breaks in the flow of events open a veritable playground, a basis for new engagements. They decenter the taken-for-granted main feature by exposing its background, its *un*performed dimensions.

Such exposures challenge not only our static notion of preliminar-

---

[9] Ibid., p. 23.

[10] Bertolt Brecht, *Brecht on Theatre* (New York: Hill and Wang, 1964), pp. 227–28.

ies—preparations, warm-ups, foreplays, rehearsals—but also our sense of where things will end. They detach us from the reality of our defenses, facades, frames, and formalities, as in a performance Richard Schechner staged when, as director of "Commune," he asked a group of students to show up before its scheduled opening:

> About ten students showed up, and they entered the theater together with the performers. The visitors were to go wherever they pleased. They watched warmups, listened to notes, helped the tech director check the lights, set the props, fill the tub, clean up the theater. They watched the performers put on their costumes and saw the regular audience arrive at 7:45. Then the performance. After, the routine of closing up the theater for the night: removing costumes and putting them in the laundry bag for washing, re-collecting props. . . . The performers were a little uneasy at their presence for warmups and notes. After the performance no one minded who was there. I felt funny too and performed a little for the "real-time" audience. . . . Removing the "magic" from the theater won't be easy.[11]

Schechner's act breaks the idealized conception of theater by depriving it of its magic, just as novels, journalism, films, and poems are broken when their generic limits are frankly acknowledged within their contours. By explicitly reflecting on their genre, on their specific techniques and conventions, such aesthetic practices in fact do more than call attention to their limitations, their partisanship and incompleteness. They also redeem our determination to impose a stable cognitive conceptual order on the ever-shifting perceptual flux by clarifying that without it we could not manage to see.

TO BREAK UP performances which have become comfortable embodiments of our expectations inevitably makes life more complicated. Aliens enter when marriages open to illicit relationships or classrooms to unex-

---

[11] Richard Schechner, *Environmental Theater* (New York: Hawthorne Books, 1973), p. 75.

pected practices. How the disruptions of familiar scenes make room for the new is especially dramatized in films that digress from their ostensible subject matter. Their cutting into the easy continuity of the featured story extends the plot lines—as when in *Missouri Breaks* Jack Nicholson climbs down a wooden railway tressle and abruptly stops to remove a splinter that had lodged in his hand. It is an arresting, yet utterly inconsequential shot that adds nothing to the story even as it reminds its audience that there is more to life than projected by an unbroken film. When in *Heartland* the casket of Rip Torn's newborn son is about to be lowered, Rip Torn abruptly brushes some soil off its cover—and we are suddenly moved. At the end of Fellini's *Amarcord* the grandfather rushes up a hill to join his family for a picnic when, *for no reason,* he pauses to pull up one of his socks. And far more oddly, Marleen Gorris's *Question of Silence* upsets audience expectations by leaving unexplained why three sane, ordinary women kill a sane, ordinary shopkeeper whom they know as little as they know one another. He's done nothing specific to offend them: he's merely male. There's no logic, no male logic, to their act: the women aren't getting even for some identifiable abuse. The invisible rage they share is but their way of interacting with the way things are, with the way men are in the existing order of things. There's no cause, no plan, no preparation. When the prosecutor at their trial compares their crime with three men *conspiring* to kill a woman, they simply break into laughter. Such focused logic is beyond them: it's comic. There's nothing to be said, and Marleen Gorris doesn't have them explain. Like women in the audience who, too, burst out laughing, their laughter fills the space left by the director. It interprets their speechlessness.

Their no-man's-land constitutes the entire landscape of Jean-Marie Straub's *Not Reconciled,* a movie which wholly deflates conventional dialogue. The actors speak in a voice so flat that the audience must choose between being bored or inventing undisplayed feelings and implicit continuities. Nothing is emphasized, nothing finally reconciled. The actors are passively quoting lines from an invisible script. Betraying no emotions, they leave part of the acting to the audience. As one reviewer, Melanie Magisos, has noted, the viewers are not "living the events as actors do in traditional Hollywood films; there is no attempt to trick the viewer into believing that the situations are reality. Dialogue is delivered in monotone;

it is chanted by the actors almost like a litany. The characters go through their actions slowly and with no emotion, like machines. Facial expressions are neutral even in what should be climactic moments."[12] The same emptiness is elaborately staged in Ingmar Bergman's *Persona* (1966). At its climax the movie abruptly stops, goes up in flames, and leaves the screen white. Previously the audience had witnessed the growing friendship between Elizabeth, an actress who has lost her power of speech, and Alma, her nurse. One evening Alma confides to her patient that she had once been involved in a day and night of sex on a beach. She recalls her nakedness and her pleasure, and she adds that she has never told anyone else. Later Alma discovers that Elizabeth had written her husband how "interesting" it was to have a nurse as an object of study. Resenting her having merely been an object of Elizabeth's curiosity, Alma places a fragment of glass in Elizabeth's path and watches Elizabeth cutting her foot. At that point Alma's and Elizabeth's eyes meet, the screen turns white, the movie has ruptured. It has broken as decisively as the relationship between the two women, as the relationship between the audience and what had been a smoothly flowing narrative. Whatever surfaces are featured in Bergman's *Persona,* the film reveals their incompleteness. It won't say it all, and thus makes the audience sit up, become reflective, and question the supposed inevitability of plot development, what D. H. Lawrence called "the fatal chain of continuity" in one of his stories.

In Luigi Pirandello's novel *The Late Mattia Pascal* (1921), the central character envisages a production of *Electra,* the very play in which *Persona*'s Elizabeth had acted and during which she had fallen silent. It is performed in a marionette theater. The character asks about a hole in the sky:

> What would happen if at the climax, when the marionette playing Orestes is about to avenge the death of his father, if at that very moment the paper sky of the theater would be rent apart? . . . Orestes would be terribly disconcerted by that hole in the sky, . . . he would continue to feel the impulse to punish, he would want to follow through with passionate

---

[12] Melanie Magisos, "*Not Reconciled:* The Destruction of Narrative Pleasure," *Wide Angle* 3 (Winter 1980): 35.

> actions, but his eyes would move to that tear and remain fixed there. . . . Happy are the marionettes above whose wooden heads the artificial sky remains unbroken. . . . And they can go about their business bravely and enjoy the comedy they are playing . . . without ever feeling dizzy or faint.

Happy are the marionettes under the unbroken sky; happy are the audiences in the seamless routines of their life. But once made to lose their footing they can recover only by providing their own response to the design of the play. They must commence to act, to express themselves, to relate what has been broken, to engage in acts of symbolizing, making whole, healing. They must emerge as actors writing their own script.

Thus scripts and their authors lose their power in works that refer to themselves. Truffaut's *Day for Night,* Resnais's *Providence,* Fellini's *8 ½,* Reisz's *French Lieutenant's Woman,* Rush's *Stuntman,* and Godard's *Passion* all raise questions about the camera's place. As the point of view drifts, the audience is nudged toward an unstable world of make-believe. The film which itself presents a film becomes as much of a performance as the film it presents, so that ultimately no reality remains behind the array of presentations and performances. *The French Lieutenant's Woman* (in which the smooth narrative of the 1860s is repeatedly dismantled by the camera's sudden focus on the same actors in the 1980s) alerts audiences to the possibility that the portrayal of the 1980s, however real it seems, is not the last word—and that off-screen there is but an infinite expanse of recycled performances. Les Blank's *Burden of Dreams,* which documents the making of Herzog's *Fitzcarraldo,* invites further interpretations of *Fitzcarraldo,* which is Herzog's reworking of a myth of entrepreneurial obsession. Chris Marker's *A.K.,* which documents the production of Akira Kurosawa's *Ran,* features Kurosawa as commanding general who cajoles, supports, and reprimands his troops, lifting the burden of his dreams. As endings are suspended in films that overlap and recognize one another, beginnings fade as well. *The Great Northfield Minnesota Raid* pays homage to a whole series of films which, for the moment, are grounded in an unrealized project—presumably *The Really Real Jesse James Story.*

In *The Clowns,* the camera pulls back to show Fellini directing *The Clowns;* he emerges as an actor who responds to the cues of an invisible director—to his own off-screen self now acting as acting director. Like Wagner breaking his airtight ideology in the jagged passages of the third act of *Tristan,* Fellini keeps his romanticism from taking over: he detaches himself, enlarges the frame, and lets an absent director do the directing.

IT IS OF course easier to see events as part of a natural, unbreakable plot. At best pictures don't lie, they correspond to reality. The best documentaries will appear to be unmanipulated, natural sequences of events. They're candid, unposed. No wonder, then, that nonprofessionals who have been recruited to act in movies don't think of themselves as actors engaged in inventing reality, themselves, and their careers. They're "naturals." In a documentary about the making of *One Flew over the Cuckoo's Nest* the professional nurses and doctors who played the parts of nurses and doctors recalled how their previous experience prepared them to act—so that they scarcely needed to act. Ignoring that they had survived the testing of graduate schools—veritable screen tests—in order to act as professional nurses and doctors in hospitals and clinics, they said that their film performance was easy—simply doing what comes naturally. Absorbed by their routines, they had no ground for recalling that they themselves had enacted them: their lives were their own ground for being.

When this ground is broken it becomes possible to gain a point of view that deprives one's career of its naturalness. Health can emerge as illness, solutions as problems, backgrounds as foregrounds. The world becomes pliable and slippery, and we realize it's up to us to conceptualize our experience, construct our existence, enact our lives. Engaged by those ground-breaking ventures in which magicians, shamans, actors, and artists take the lead, we can appreciate Gordon Matta-Clark's disconcerting projects, his "cuttings" of various architectural structures—the New Jersey house he sawed in half in a project he called "Splitting" (1974), his "Office Baroque" (1977) in Antwerp, his "Circus" (1978) in Chicago. He split a wall in 1974 and entitled it Bingo. In a Paris gallery, he exhibited a hole he dug through its floor. Such exploits merit recognition because they turn out to arouse passive observers and draw them into the artist's transgressions—as Mallarmé's poetry leads his readers through varied typefaces into the blank spaces he prescribed for the typographical layouts of his poems or as Cornelius Cardew's musical scores open possibilities for comprehending experiences that are deleted from conventional musical notations:

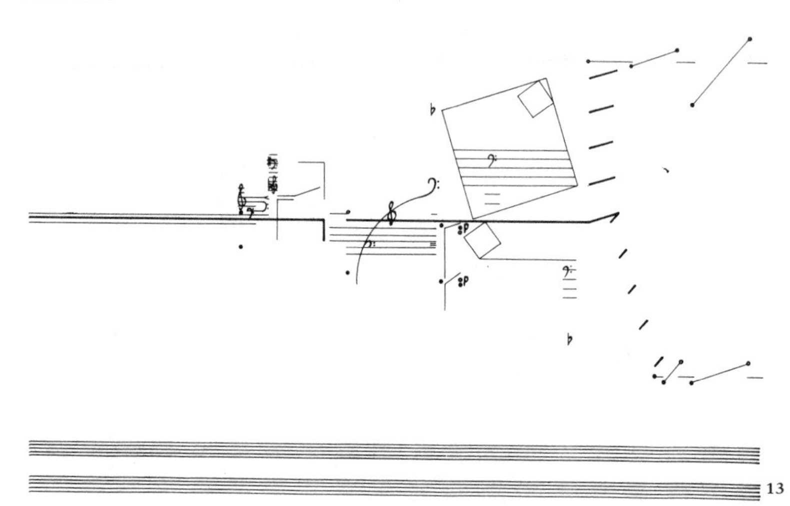
[13]

Reviewing Part VI of "The Great Learning," a collection of Cardew's pieces for various ensembles, Tom Johnson has noted how the score makes room finally for "the last and slowest singer":

> Scored for a cappella chorus, it asks each singer to sing fragments of the text on notes of their own choosing. Each fragment is repeated a specific number of times, one breath per note. When performed by a fairly large chorus, the result can produce amazing semitonal harmonies and lovely choral textures, even with amateur singers and no rehearsal. In the beginning everyone sings the same words, but as the piece goes on, the fast breathers move ahead of the slow breathers, meaning that several chunks of text are then heard at the same time. The ending can be quite poignant as the fast breathers finish and drop out, and the music tapers off. The piece often ends with a solo, as the last and slowest singer patiently completes the final lines.[14]

---

[13] Cornelius Cardew, *Treatise* (Buffalo, N.Y.: Gallery Upstairs Press, 1967), © 1967.

[14] Tom Johnson, "Cornelius Cardew, 1936–1981," *Village Voice*, May 18, 1982, p. 79.

The disruption of musical conventions opens Cardew's work to "the last and slowest singer."[15] His performance is like Francis Huxley's *Raven and the Writing Desk* (1982), which accepts Lewis Carroll's *Alice in Wonderland* only to fragment it by subverting the conventions of critical analysis.[16] His re-imaging of Alice's adventures is achieved by crossing conceptual wires—puns that relate everything to everything else. Huxley keeps inquiring "in depth," as he says, into the meaning of Lewis Carroll's famous unanswered riddle: "Why is a raven like a writing desk?" Yet by relating the riddle to the fragments of Carroll's life—his mathematics, symbolic logic, religion, family, and sexual preoccupations—Huxley's sheer versatility decenters the logic of scholarly orthodoxy. Nonsense, Huxley explains in one of the book's few sober passages, is "a logical game played with feeling by at least two people, in a spirit of self-contradiction, in such a way that one thing leads on to the other to the constant surprise and mutual enthusiasm of both parties." By abandoning common sense and relating unrelated things nonsense communicates in ways discredited by a logic that forbids the infinite convertibility of whatever we know to be the case. Nonsense sustains the kind of conversation that lightly trips from topic to topic and never does answer the riddle why a raven is like a writing desk. To say, as Huxley proposes, that "Poe wrote on both" is to imply that the last word is not in. It is to deny that a writer is a writer, a book a book, or a chest of drawers (as in René Magritte's visual pun) a chest of drawers. Huxley lets word leak out that nothing *is*, that nothing

---

[15] "Any expressive form works (when it works) by disarranging semantic contexts in such a way that properties conventionally ascribed to certain things are unconventionally ascribed to others, which are then seen actually to possess them. To call the wind a cripple, as Stevens does, to fix tone and manipulate timbre, as Schoenberg does, or, closer to our case, to picture an art critic as a dissolute bear, as Hogarth does, is to cross conceptual wires; the established conjunctions between objects and their qualities are altered and phenomena—fall weather, melodic shape or cultural journalism—are clothed in signifiers which normally point to other referents." (Clifford Geertz, *Local Knowledge* [New York: Basic Books, 1983], p. 234.)

[16] Francis Huxley, *The Raven and the Writing Desk* (New York: Harper & Row, 1982). Julian Barnes's hybrid of a novel, *Flaubert's Parrot* (New York: Knopf, 1985), is similarly inventive. See also Michael Fried, *Realism, Writing, Disfiguration: On Thomas Eakins and Stephen Crane* (Chicago: University of Chicago Press, 1987).

makes a *real* difference, that the only defensible careers or texts are those which reject ontologies by acknowledging the endless duplicitousness of reality.

And yet Huxley remains in Lewis Carroll's world even as he dissolves it. He stays as much in touch with his subject as Jacques Derrida stays in touch with Shelley's "Triumph of Life," in a way concisely reviewed by Christopher Norris:

> He makes no pretense of "interpreting" the poem but uses its title and random associative hints as a springboard into regions of giddying uncertainty, where details merge and cross in a joyful breakdown of all proprietory limits. Any talk of meaning or structure is ineluctably "caught up in a process which it does not control," which for Derrida signals the total dissolution of those boundaries that mark off one text from another, or that try to interpose between poem and commentary. "The Triumph of Life" is teasingly played off against Blanchot's narrative *L'Arrêt de mort,* producing a series of figurative crossings and wild substitutions which abolish all sense of textual autonomy. This gambit is pushed to the limit by a footnote, addressed to the translator, which runs the full length of Derrida's text and constantly adverts to the impossible nature of the whole undertaking—the way in which translation exemplifies the "abysmal" slippages and detours of all understanding.[17]

Here and elsewhere Derrida frees himself even as he remains in a circle in which interpretations endlessly mirror interpretations, in which new interpretations are but new strategies for redeeming texts made stale by established courses of literature.

Derrida's tactics for displacing the dead weight of tradition are no less those of Evangeline Tabasco's meticulously mounted collection of discarded bottle openers, nuts, bolts, and washers under the title of "Splendors of the Sohites," her project for redeeming the city's discarded artifacts. Similarly the graffiti, sidewalk stencils, and lurid posters which erupted in New York City in the 1980s introduced not only new talent but also new forms for bringing private agonies into the open, for compre-

---

[17] Christopher Norris, *Deconstruction: Theory and Practice* (New York: Methuen, 1982), pp. 114–15.

hending the city's submerged pain, its belt of arson, its slums, garbage, waste, and raunchiness. Marshall Berman's reaction to the devastation wreaked in New York City by Robert Moses's imperious schemes of development has the same function. In the concluding part of his study defining the experience of modernity, Berman inquired how one might comprehend and salvage the urban landscape.[18] He sought both to accept and to transcend the prevailing ugliness, specifically his own streets of the Bronx. Advocating dramatic displays of symbols wherever waves of pain remain unsymbolized, looking for symbols to *contain* the unexpressed malaise of modernization, he projected his fantasy:

> The Bronx Mural, as I imagine it, would be painted onto the brick and concrete retaining walls that run alongside most of the eight miles of the Cross-Bronx Expressway, so that every automobile trip through and out of the Bronx would become a trip into its buried depths. In the places where the road runs close to or above ground level, and the walls recede, the driver's view of the Bronx's past life would alternate with sweeping vistas of its present ruin. The mural might depict cross-sections of streets, of houses, even of rooms full of people just as they were before the Expressway cut through them all.
>
> But it would go back before this, to our century's early years, at the height of the Jewish and Italian immigration, with the Bronx growing along the rapidly expanding subway lines, and (in the words of the *Communist Manifesto*) whole populations conjured out of the ground: to tens of thousands of garment workers, printers, butchers, house painters, furriers, union militants, socialists, anarchists, communists. Here is D. W. Griffith, whose old Biograph Studio building still stands, solid but battered and neglected, at the Expressway's edge; here is Sholem Aleichem, seeing the New World and saying that it was good, and dying on Kelly Street (the block where Bella Abzug was born); and there is Trotsky on East 164th Street, waiting for his revolution (did he really play a Russian in obscure silent films? We will never know). Now we see a modest but energetic and

---

[18] Marshall Berman, *All That Is Solid Melts into Air: The Experience of Modernity* (New York: Simon & Schuster, 1982), pp. 341–43. For a splendid discourse which salvages and reconstructs New York City more elaborately, see Peter Conrad, *The Art of the City: Views and Versions of New York* (New York: Oxford University Press, 1984).

confident bourgeoisie, springing up in the 1920s near the new Yankee Stadium, promenading on the Grand Concourse for a brief moment in the sun, finding romance in the swan boats in Crotona Park; and not far away, "the coops," a great network of workers' housing settlements, cooperatively building a new world beside Bronx and Van Cortlandt parks. We move on to the bleak adversity of the 1930s, unemployment lines, home relief, the WPA (whose splendid monument, the Bronx County Courthouse, stands just above the Yankee Stadium), radical passions and energies exploding, street-corner fights between Trotskyites and Stalinists, candy stores and cafeterias ablaze with talk all through the night; then to the excitement and anxiety of the postwar years, new affluence, neighborhoods more vibrant than ever, even as new worlds beyond the neighborhoods begin to open up, people buy cars, start to move; to the Bronx's new immigrants from Puerto Rico, South Carolina, Trinidad, new shades of skin and clothes on the street, new music and rhythms, new tensions and intensities; and finally, to Robert Moses and his dread road, smashing through the Bronx's inner life, transforming evolution into devolution, entropy into catastrophe, and creating the ruin on which this work of art is built.

The mural would have to be executed in a number of radically different styles, so as to express the amazing variety of imaginative visions that sprang from these apparently uniform streets, apartment houses, school yards, kosher butcher shops, appetizing and candy stores. Barnett Newman, Stanley Kubrick, Clifford Odets, Larry Rivers, George Segal, Jerome Weidman, Rosalyn Drexler, E. L. Doctorow, Grace Paley, Irving Howe, would all be there; along with George Meany, Herman Badillo, Bella Abzug and Stokely Carmichael; John Garfield, Tony Curtis' Sidney Falco, Gertrude Berg's Molly Goldberg, Bess Myerson (an iconic monument to assimilation, the Bronx's Miss America, 1945), and Anne Bancroft; Hank Greenberg, Jake La Motta, Jack Molinas (Was he the Bronx's greatest athlete, its most vicious crook, or both?); Nate Archibald; A. M. Rosenthal of the *New York Times* and his sister, the communist leader Ruth Witt; Phil Spector, Bill Graham, Dion and the Belmonts, the Rascals, Laura Nyro, Larry Harlow, the brothers Palmieri; Jules Feiffer and Lou Meyers; Paddy Chayevsky and Neil Simon; Ralph Lauren and Calvin Klein, Garry Winogrand, George and Mike Kuchar; Jonas Salk, George Wald, Seymour Melman, Herman Kahn—all these, and so many more.

> Children of the Bronx would be encouraged to return and put themselves in the picture: the Expressway wall is big enough to hold them all; as it got increasingly crowded, it would approach the density of the Bronx at its peak. To drive past and through all this would be a rich and strange experience. Drivers might feel captivated by the figures, environments and fantasies on the mural, ghosts of their parents, their friends, even of themselves, like sirens enticing them to plunge into the abyss of the past. On the other hand, so many of these ghosts would be urging and driving them on, dying to leap into a future beyond the Bronx's walls and join the stream of traffic on the way out. The Bronx Mural would end at the end of the Expressway itself, where it interchanges on the way to Westchester and Long Island. The end, the boundary between the Bronx and the world, would be marked with a gigantic ceremonial arch, in the tradition of the colossal monuments that Claes Oldenburg conceived in the 1960s. This arch would be circular and inflatable, suggesting both an automobile tire and a bagel. When fully pumped up, it would look indigestibly hard as a bagel, but ideal as a tire for a fast getaway; when soft, it would appear leaky and dangerous as a tire but, as a bagel, inviting to settle down and eat.[19]

Berman's conception responds to Claes Oldenburg's call "for an art that embroils itself with everyday crap and comes out on top."[20] It is in line with the musical performance orchestrated by Gunnar Schonbeck as it was reported in 1976 in Bennington College's *Quadrille:*

> Gunnar Schonbeck, teacher, instrument maker and all-around music maker, inaugurated the Greenwall Music Workshop in the new Arts Center at Bennington College with an extravaganza on March 17 that involved nearly 1,000 people in seven bands, four choruses, with faculty and student ensembles of the Music Division of the College.
>
> The concert was the World Premiere of Schonbeck's "Collage No. 10," a two-hour piece involving, among other things, a revival of the Bennington College bell ringers (part of every commencement from 1936 to about 1953); speaking and-or singing solos by the acting president, Joseph

[19] Berman, *All That Is Solid,* pp. 341–43. Reprinted by permission of Georges Borchardt, Inc., © 1982 by Marshall Berman.

[20] Quoted in James Russell and Suzi Gabilib, *Pop Art Redefined* (New York: Prague, 1970), p. 97. Reprinted by permission of Georges Borchardt, Inc., © 1982 by Marshall Berman.

S. Iseman, the chairman of the Board, Merreli Hambleton, the Dean of Faculty, Reinhoud van der Linde, and Dean of Studies, Ronald Lee Cohen. They were accompanied by 40 chimes, some as long as 20 feet, some as short as three inches, 20 steel harps, 60 giant marimbas, seven bands, and an opera based on Bela Bartok's concept of a Serbo-Croation Heroic Song.

The audience was asked to sing, hum, make sounds and noises, and otherwise participate in "Collage No. 10." Schonbeck positioned the various bands, choruses, instruments and participants around the mammoth music workshop and pieced their music together in a kind of Ivesian sound collage.

Also participating were the 150-member Hoosick Falls Senior Band, the 75-member Hoosic Falls Junior Band, the 100-member Cambridge Senior Band, the Mount Greylock Symphonic Winds (90 members), the North Bennington Junior Band (40 children), the 150-voice Cambridge Central Chorus, and the 150-voice Hoosick Falls Central Chorus. Along with a 10-member Bennington College faculty ensemble, a 100-student orchestra, and some 50 guest artists.

"Collage No. 10" comes in three parts, each about the same length. The first part is called commencement, and is based on the traditional Bennington College Version of it. Bell ringers rang the virtually forgotten college alma mater song, "Bright Sing nor Sigh," written the second semester by a student in 1933. Chimes were played and various people spoke as part of the beginning celebration of the new Arts Center.

The second part is the opera. It is based on the Serbo-Croation Heroic Song entitled "The Captivity of Dulic Ibrahim." The narrator was drama instructor Leroy Logan, and Richard Frisch, baritone, and Barabara Stein Mallow, cellist, performed solos. Several of the choruses and Bennington faculty and student musicians also participated.

The finale involved every participant and member of the audience. Each band and chorus had five minutes in which to play whatever it wanted and Schonbeck pulled it all together in his aural collage. The audience hummed, the marimbas, steel drums and a hammer dulcimer ensemble accompanied while Gunnar Schonbeck whirled in the midst of it all, like an itinerant alchemist pulling the sound out of anything and everyone present.

However conventional the musical pieces appropriated by Schonbeck, the context he provided made them newly accessible. Similarly, John Cage's musical celebration of James Joyce's centenary, "Roaratorio," became what Cage aptly called a circus. Wilfrid Mellers has remembered one of its performances:

> As he reads [randomly selected passages from *Finnegans Wake*]—and the intonations of his voice are themselves music—the audience circumnavigates the auditorium, picking-up now one, now another, of the sound-strands emitted by multiple electrophonic speakers. The tapes "superimpose seventy-two layers of sound from places mentioned in the Wake." The babel of bars, the yells of babies, cats and dogs, amorous or murderous cries in the night, the girglings of the river Liffey and what could be (who but Cage knows?) the bubbling of vats of Guinness assail our ears, making the environment within which we live, move and, "for the Time being," have our Being. Though we are not called upon to make choices between these sounds, there is a further aural dimension which complicates the situation. It is this complication that makes the total experience richly rewarding.
>
> Dotted around the hall are a number of live musicians, representatives of Irish folk culture: a singer, a fiddler, a flute-player, a piper, two drummers. These folk musicians intermittently create their "musics of necessity" which spring from the lives they've led in the contexts of tradition but which, *going on,* become at once historical and eternally present. What they make is not the artifacts of Western "works" of art but a *continuum,* existing within the flux we're surrounded by. That they endure makes our awareness of chaos peculiarly poignant.[21]

The groundbreaking process in which new structures are enacted is familiar—Cage reintegrating the episodes of *Finnegans Wake,* Joyce those of Ulysses, Berman those of New York City's past constructions. Such play is precisely what transpires in the project Richard Schechner has called Collage Theater:

> Cage, that Johnny Appleseed of the arts, first planted the idea of multifocus and collage theater in my head. . . . The idea did not start then; it was everywhere: in Happenings, Events, and Activities, in music and dance, in Op Art—all mixtures of camp and virility, fad and authentic impulse. The

---

[21] Wilfrid Mellers, "John Cage at Seventy," *London Times Literary Supplement,* June 11, 1982, p. 637.

> "static arts" were beginning to exist actively in time; and as they were becoming theatricalized, theater was sure to reciprocate. . . .
>
> I was standing in an intersection, and conflicting traffic was everywhere, and yet my art was going nowhere. And I thought of "radical" in its original, literal sense: what was the "root" of theater and how could I (at least theoretically) redirect it? The roots of theater are the audience and the play. Everything else—actors, directors, stage—serves these two things. If theater was to be changed, the audience and the plays would have to be altered. But change meant more than simply getting new audiences and new plays which, after all, would be very much like the old. And since people do not change (light-footed biology is slow-moving), the task was to make people use faculties they do not now use in theatergoing: a perceptual re-education. As for plays, they had to be thought of as something other than they had been. But before that "other" could emerge, the theater literature that was there had to be removed. The great classics no longer refreshed me; instead they were formidable obstacles.

Schechner goes on:

> One changes the audience's perceptions by removing that central focus which has had their attention from the beginning. No seats, no single action, no inert buildings, no attempt to direct their eyes and ears. Leave the work of selection and focus to them. Shock them not by offering cruel, singular images, but by sending such a multiplicity of visual and aural messages that the basic experience-structuring is forced on them. Go beyond medieval and circus theater. Duplicate the number and approximate the kind of messages sent on Piccadilly at rush hour. Analyze and disintegrate sight and sound somewhat as the first cubists did to two-dimensional vision. Destroy theater's melody line which is the story; but do it more effectively than Ionesco ever did in his "planned chaos" of *The Bald Prima Donna*. Make it all not a sentimental cry against a complex world, but a celebration of the world's complexity.
>
> For example. Take a large, nearly square room. Examine its architecture and plan whatever follows in relation to it. Choose a room that even when empty is visually interesting. Bring a crowd in. Begin in one corner to play a scene from *Hamlet*. The people press close to see and hear. When their attention is focused, play Beethoven's Seventh Symphony over fifteen

> or twenty loud-speakers: *Hamlet* becomes pantomime, though the actors are still speaking. Then, somewhere else in the room, do a scene from *The Importance of Being Earnest.* In comes the chorus from *The Oresteia,* usurping space for its chants and dances. Moving among audience and performers are several jugglers. Overhead, projected on large screens, are movies of this very scene as it occurred the night before, or the week before: a canopy which is a mirror. The sounds and sights modulate, increase in tempo, vary in intensity; spatial figurations also change—performances impinge upon each other and the spectators. The spectators impinge back. We make a classic collage—we treat the old texts as material, not as model. And we introduce into the interior of the building some approximation of the busyness that fills the outside.
>
> This classic collage is, of course, only one example. There could be modern collages or mixtures. Performances would be unstructured or structured, but always the individual spectator would be asked to choose his own perspective, assemble his own images. Shows would be rehearsed (for there is a difference between an unstructured performance and happenstance). When we have destroyed the silly awe which a literary culture attaches to its books, we could again begin to make plays.
>
> What they would be like I have no idea. But the destructive process itself, like abstract expressionism in painting, would be a most constructive phase in theater history.[22]

The events featured by Schechner's theater are less important than his design of a structure that simultaneously holds and dissolves them. Engaged in acts of integrating and relating, he decenters what threatens to become polarized—specific performances, plotlines, genres. His preoccupations are those of any artist who presumes to restructure the finalities of our lives—Philip Glass's theater pieces which combine dance, storytelling, instrumental music, and vocal music no less than Stanley Elkin's novels which bring the dead ends of our lives into settings that redeem them.

Eschewing naturalistic plots that impose coherence, sequences, and epiphanies, Elkin in particular has opened free-for-all ground for the

---

22 Richard Schechner, as quoted in Henry Kariel, *The Political Order* (New York: Free Press, 1970), pp. 3–5.

proliferation of episodes, anecdotes, speeches, fantasies, analogies, arias, melodramas, nonsequiturs, travelogues, newscasts, catalogs, and jokes—a flashy kaleidoscope, an extemporaneous, lavish display of an aggressive, forbidden, virtually autonomous language spoken by no identifiable narrator. "But life's tallest order," he has commented, "is to keep the feelings up, to make the two dollars worth of euphoria go the distance. And life can't do that. So fiction does."[23] To make euphoria go the distance, Elkin would seem to let nothing go to waste. Like Whitman, he is excessive, self-indulgent, omnivorous. Looking at the world unblinkingly, Elkin risks exhaustion by treating nothing as alien, vulgar, or wild. In a democratic dance which, as his titles have it, is "the living end," a "search and seizure," he equalizes whatever he grabs. Everything is touched by his "poetics for bullies" (another title). He wallows in imagist extravagance—magic rhetoric at the edge of disease and death, linguistic cascades, verbal avalanches that grow as they descent, all an exhibit of energy which, in the lives of Elkin's characters, become the more intense the closer they move toward their end. In his words, "there is an inverse ratio between small cause for joy and joy's expression."[24] He prods his galloping metaphors to "upset the applecarts of expectation and ordinary grammar."[25] A ubiquitous voice consolidates the subject matter of his books even as it testifies to his refusal to be reconciled.

Elkin's fiction is sustained by his unwillingness to say the last word. It treats everyone and everything as a restless, fleeting appearance to be captured by a restless, fleeting structure. Whatever appears is like the reversible figures of Escher's familiar graphics—nothing but a continuously exciting narrating medium. Escher's work, too, inhabits a space that has no center, projecting the same nonstructure which Gerald Holton, a philosopher of science, has seen to emerge in contemporary physics:

> The reigning themata until about the mid-nineteenth century have been expressed most characteristically by the mandala of a static, homocentric,

---

[23] Stanley Elkin, "Introduction," *The Best American Short Stories 1980* (New York: Houghton Mifflin, 1980), pp. xviii–xix.

[24] Stanley Elkin, review of Malamud, *The Fixer*, in *Massachusetts Review* 8 (Spring 1967): 389–90.

[25] Elkin, quoted by Scott Sanders, "An Interview with Stanley Elkin," *Contemporary Literature* 16 (Spring 1975): 133.

> hierarchically ordered, harmoniously arranged cosmos, rendered in sharply delineated lines as in those of Copernicus' own handwriting. . . . This representation was slowly supplanted by another, increasingly so in the last half of the 19th century. The universe became unbounded, "restless" (to use a fortunate description of Max Born), a weakly coupled ensemble of infinitely many separate, individually sovereign parts and events. . . . The clear lines of the earlier mandala have been replaced by undelineated, fuzzy smear. . . . And now, a significant number of our most thoughtful scholars seem to fear that a third mandala is rising to take precedence over both of these—the labyrinth with the empty center, where the investigator meets only his own shadow.[26]

It is this postmodernist mandala which guided Stanley Edgar Hyman's *The Tangled Bank* (1959), a groundbreaking review of Darwin, Marx, Frazer, and Freud as "mere" narrators. Hyman made it valid for Gillian Beer to appreciate Darwin's prodigiously tangled narrative as planting nothing final in the ground it broke:

> Darwinian theory will not resolve to a single significance nor yield a single pattern. It is essentially multivalent. It renounces a Descartian clarity, or univocality. Darwin's methods of argument and the generative metaphors of *The Origins* lead . . . into profusion and extension. The unused, or uncontrolled elements in metaphors such as "the struggle for existence" take on life of their own. They surpass their status in the text and generate further ideas and ideologies. They include "more than the maker of them at the time knew."[27]

Whatever the reservations of social scientists in quest of empirically secured explanations, Hans Peter Duerr has cheerfully injected the narratives of positivist anthropology into a structure he calls dreamtime, a time which gives equal status to the austere rationality of science and the evocative imagery of elusive mythologies. An appreciative critic, Joseph

---

[26] Gerald Holton, *Science and Culture* (Boston: Houghton Mifflin, 1965), pp. xxviii–xxix.

[27] Gillian Beer, *Darwin's Plot* (London: Routledge & Kegan Paul, 1983), p. 9. See also L. J. Jordanova, ed., *Languages of Nature: Critical Essays on Science and Literature* (New Brunswick, N.J.: Rutgers University Press, 1986).

Agassi, has noted how Duerr lives on the fence like shamans and magicians, how he makes his readers work while simultaneously offering them the fruits of his anthropological labor:

> He is constantly on the move, sees all sorts of connections, significant or trite; he sparkles whenever he can; he points at the sense of wonder, at the yearning, at the unity with nature which pseudo-scientific hostility makes us ignore; he observes that science is limited, that it, too is an unending quest. . . . [B]ut what the end-product is I cannot say. . . . There is no clear specific purpose, except purpose of peace, of peace of mind, of wholeness.[28]

The landscape and the time made meaningful by Duerr is shared by John Cage, who too offers no end-products, who makes no move to organize dances, to encourage patriotic fervor, to stimulate cows being milked or people being led to fill their carts in supermarkets. His music is radically useless; his renowned pauses are eerie settings for melodies his audiences might compose. What they hear when Cage's score provides for four minutes and thirty seconds during which the pianist is to sit immobile at a piano is what remains unsaid in a conversation that has abruptly ceased. Like the intensive gaze of lovers, such silences offer a chance to construct new worlds. Our unfocused purposefulness becomes the ground on which to relate the particular episodes of our lives, of whatever befalls us. We express unheard elements of ourselves and vacillate like Falstaff, forever changing so as to connect with subdued parts of ourselves.

THE RELEVANCE OF Falstaff's character is made evident by Jonas Barish's study, *The Antitheatrical Prejudice* (1981). He has noted how Falstaff especially provides "a positive version of the phenomenon of self-change, a glimpse into its transfiguring possibilities." Falstaff is the embodiment of limitless transformation:

> Without a trade, without a family, without plans or projects, without a past or a future, contemptuous of consistency, he lives exclusively in the present by a chameleonlike adjustment to the needs of the moment. Past and future,

---

[28] Joseph Agassi, review of Hans Peter Duerr, *Traumzeit* (1978), in *Inquiry* 24 (Spring 1987): 462, 469.

> plans and projects imply a part of a regular pattern, a submission, in some measure, to a restriction of one's identity. Falstaff bows to no rule other than that of his pleasure and appetite. Since he possesses no certain identity, he must create one anew at every moment, largely by wit. It is useless to tax him with a tale of what he is here and now, what he makes of himself under the stimulus of persons and events. Taxed with his poltroonery of yesterday, he replies by inventing out of whole cloth—buckram of Kendall green—the hero of today. Hence our odd sensation that his explanations are *irrelevant*. They refer to a past that has no meaning for him, or at least, which he is continually rewriting to make conform to his present needs.[29]

The playwright himself is but an actor, that ideal poet whom Baudelaire saw enjoying "the incomparable privilege of being, at will, both himself and other people. Like a wandering soul seeking a body, he can enter, whenever he wishes, into anyone's personality."[30] He is Le Carré's perfect spy, Magnus Pym, who betrays all he loves, believes he is nothing ("entirely put together from bits of other people, poor fellow"), speeding in overdrive to remain all things to all people. No positivist, the actor is the poet who cultivates negative capability, as Keats wrote in a celebrated letter. His is a capacity for "being in uncertainties, mysteries, doubts, without any irritable reaching after fact." A person without positive qualities, he has no identity. He is Thomas Mann's Felix Krull, who confesses that he "masqueraded in both cases, and the undisguised reality behind the two appearances, the real I, could not be determined because it did not actually exist."[31] His life is Woody Allen's in *Zelig* (1983)—an ongoing crisis, a permanent readiness to become someone else. However familiar, Keats's words remain telling:

> As to the poetical Character itself it is not itself . . . it has no self—it is everything and nothing—it has no character—it enjoys light and shade; it

[29] Jonas Barish, *The Antitheatrical Prejudice* (Berkeley and Los Angeles: University of California Press, 1981), pp. 128–30.

[30] Charles Baudelaire, *Letters* (Cambridge: Harvard University Press, 1958), pp. 386–87.

[31] Thomas Mann, *The Confessions of Felix Krull, Confidence Man* (Frankfurt: S. Fischer, 1954), p. 266.

> lives in gusto, be it foul or fair, high or low, rich or poor, mean or elevated—It has as much delight in conceiving an Iago as an Imogen. . . . A Poet is the most unpoetical of anything in existence; because he has no Identity—he is continually in for—and filling some other Body—The Sun, the Moon, the Sea and Men and Women who are creatures of impulse are poetical and have about them an unchangeable attribute—the poet has none; no identity.[32]

The poet's ever-drifting self allows him to play the roles of others. As Melville's Ishmael or Mann's Felix Krull, the quintessential performer moves lightly through manifold roles and tells the heavy tale—*survives* to tell the tale. He's shifty and keeps moving. Never quite conforming to what is expected of him, he is like the Kabuki actor whose discipline forbids him to construct his individualistic Real Self. At its most intense his act is, strictly speaking, no *self*-expression, no *self*-presentation. Not seeking to make some preexisting interior self-structure visible, "he" (the pronoun must appear in quotes) maneuvers within structures, texts, and languages which impinge on him. Whether engaged in chess, mountain climbing, bookkeeping, or Christmas shopping, he keeps reality at bay. What matters to him is neither what he is nor what he does but how he's doing. As he wears his mask he expects his own distinctive self to disappear. Self-effacing, he is not present: private parts of the body become public and participate.

Without enduring attachments, he remains loyal to the kingdom of love for all Being, filled with the knowledge that his world is at once the best and the worst of all possible ones, and that full assent to it constitutes salvation. He responds to the conflicting claims of the world not by conforming to some established code but by taking his bearings every single instance, by relating to whatever he might encounter. His consciousness is that which Henry James embodied in one of his characters, Lord Mellifont:

> He directed the conversation by gestures as irresistible as they were vague; one felt as if without him it wouldn't have had anything to call a tone. This

[32] John Keats, *Letters*, ed. Hyder Edward Rollins (Cambridge: Harvard University Press, 1958), vol. 1, pp. 380–87.

> was essentially what he contributed to any occasion—what he contributed above all to English public life. He pervaded it, he coloured it, he embellished it, and without him it would have lacked, comparatively speaking, a vocabulary. Certainly it wouldn't have had a style, for a style was what it had in having Lord Mellifont. He *was* a style.[33]

It is hard, of course, to overcome one's ambivalence toward pure style—especially after reading James's equable conclusion that in whatever place Lord Mellifont had been, "the place was utterly empty . . . he had ceased to be." Troubled by this very sensibility, Robert Jay Lifton was to question those who might wish to conduct "an interminable series of experiments and explorations, some shallow, some profound, each of which can readily be abandoned in favor of still new psychological quests."[34] Lifton's uneasiness about such amoral posturing—such acting—betrays an understandable anxiety in the face of the absence of some firm nucleus. Still, Henry James had managed to remain composed enough. Confident that the web he spun would hold, not doubting *his* power, he risked dissolving in the intricacy of his refinements. Seemingly dispassionate, exiled from the gritty texture of experience, he allowed his passion to find expression in the *care* he took to pause and punctuate, to regard anything as well enough to be left alone. He thus freed his characters (and himself) so that they might display characteristics that would appear to be real. He allowed their (and his) detachment to increase, allowed Otherness to make its appearance and participate. Thus he made room for Otherness in his very self, providing a demonstration of Henry David Thoreau's account of the act of thinking in full consciousness:

> With thinking we may be beside ourselves in a sane sense. By a conscious effort of the mind we can stand aloof from actions and consequences; and all things, good and bad, go by us like a torrent. We are not wholly involved in nature. I may be either driftwood in the stream, or Indra in the sky looking down on it. I *may* be affected by a theatrical exhibition; on the other hand, I *may not* be affected by an actual event which appears to

---

33 "The Private Life," in Henry James, *Works* (New York: Scribner's, 1909), vol. 18, p. 227.

34 Robert Jay Lifton, *Boundaries* (New York: Random House, 1970), p. 44.

> concern me much more. I only know myself as a human entity; the scene, so to speak, of thoughts and affections; and am sensible of a certain doubleness by which I can stand as remote from myself as from another. However intense my experience, I am conscious of the presence and criticism of a part of me which, as it were, is not a part of me, but spectator, sharing no experience, but taking note of it: and that is no more I than it is you. When the play, it may be the tragedy, of life is over, the spectator goes his way. It was a kind of fiction, a work of the imagination only, so far as he was concerned. This doubleness may easily make us poor neighbors and friends sometimes.[35]

At the end of his autobiographical *Ways of Escape* (1982) Graham Greene paints a portrait of the Other, his other self—an imposter who calls himself "Graham Greene," who travels widely, announces himself as The Famous Writer, borrows money, makes time with women. Who exactly is he, if anyone? "I found myself shaken by a metaphysical doubt. Had *I* been the imposter all the time? Was I the Other?" Had the author lost his boundaries? Did the self become all-comprehensive? Raising questions about their own import, hinting at their inconsequence, postmodernist performances glide toward transparency—a self-negating, undifferentiated presentness in which action floats suspended.

---

[35] Henry David Thoreau, *Walden* (New York: Heritage Press, 1939), p. 140.

4 BOTTOMING OUT

ENCOUNTERING someone who does nothing but perform tends to make us shrink back and become reflective. Pauline Kael writes:

> In the shoptalk of stage and screen directors, one frequently hears about a pure actor (or actress) type—a performer who doesn't exist without the play, a sort of neurotic vacuum. Directors . . . say that this empty actor may give you a stunning performance but . . . you never know from one day to the next what attitudes he's trying on or what he'll blow up about.[1]

Screen directors are not alone in being uneasy with someone who is all masks and treats the world as theater. Thus it may be a concern for the feelings of the audience that led István Szabó, the director of *Mephisto* (1977), to present Hendrick Hofgen, who is cast as an unmitigated actor, as a morally bankrupt careerist ashamed of his conduct and eager to be punished for it (his black mistress shows up whip in hand). Insatiably

---

[1] Pauline Kael, "The Devil without Fire," *New Yorker*, May 17, 1982, pp. 128–32. Her review led me to see how unattractive the "pure actor" is made to appear in *Mephisto*.

greedy for attention, Hofgen is an unattractive presence. His sole concern is his survival as actor in the midst of the deadly machinery of Nazism—machinery to which he is sensitive precisely because it destroys the opportunity for action, "merely" because it limits and finally eliminates performances. Hofgen is shown to be too weak to extend the theatrical arena, to inspire the participation of those at the margins of the stage—whether they are the victims of Nazism or its obsessive, brutalized functionaries. The director surely knows the low tolerance of audiences for Hofgen's amoral conduct. They are not likely to applaud an actor wholly devoted to staging performances in the midst of a holocaust, wholly committed to compromising and mediating, to remaining in action whatever the context. It is but appropriate that in the brilliant final scene of *Mephisto* Hofgen is shown to collapse. He is unable to survive in the limelight: he becomes hysterical when, in the vast stadium in which a Nazi party rally is to be staged, searchlights zero in on him and he is wholly visible, wholly transparent and vulnerable, wholly devoid of substance.

Yet while we recoil from the pure actor, in wishdreams that find expression in novels we do welcome amoral characters who calmly manage to remain in action. We take pleasure in George Smiley, whose creator, John le Carré, allows him to take his bearings anew at every moment without concern for the world's distinction between good and evil. A performer in no-man's-land, Smiley is the very incarnation of the actor's disciplined alertness to opportunities for staying in motion. Whatever searchlights pursue him, he unblinkingly goes on. Alive to every ripple at the margin of his senses, he's permanently on edge. He has opted for a life that is an ongoing crisis because nothing is irrelevant. For him everything is critical—that is, normal. Without discriminating he attends as fully to evil as to good. His gaze glides; it seizes nothing. Disciplined not to sleep soundly, he is naturally near panic and exhaustion.

However high the price he pays for acting, Smiley is nevertheless so eager to go on with it that he welcomes being called out of privacy and retirement.[2] He's determined to keep performing, to play as many roles as

---

[2] In his memoirs, *On Acting* (1986), Lawrence Olivier recalls: "I was made to perform, and it is not easy to be put out to grass, left to feed on memories and friendships." Maureen Stapleton remembers being discharged: "When an actor gets fired, it's the most

necessary just to keep going, to play any role, that is, and be no one in particular. In one scene, a police superintendent takes George Smiley's measure. "Not *one* face at all actually," the superintendent reflects admiringly; "more your whole range of faces. More your patchwork of different ages, people, and endeavors." He couldn't tell what Smiley really was. "An abbey," the superintendent finally decides. "That's what he was, an abbey. . . . An abbey, made up of all sorts of conflicting ages and styles and convictions." Le Carré adds to the superintendent's thoughts:

> Smiley, he says, was not at peace; he was not, in a single phrase, definable as a single person, beyond the one constant thrust of his determination. Hunter, recluse, lover, solitary man in search of completion, shrewd player of the Great Game, avenger, doubter in search of reassurance—Smiley was by turns each one of them, and sometimes more than one.[3]

In *Smiley's People* (1980) the chief of Russia's espionage service is defeated and humiliated because he fails as actor, as role player. He is in trouble because his attachment to his schizophrenic daughter is sincere. His love for her is real—whereas for Smiley there is no abiding loyalty, no impassioned commitment, no true love. "Smiley knew that he was unled, and perhaps unleadable; that the only restraints upon him were those of his own reason, and his own humanity."[4] Like Smiley, Alec Leamas, the

---

devastating annihilating experience. It isn't just your work that you feel is being rejected, it's your whole being." (Quoted by Lillian Ross, "The Player," *New Yorker,* October 28, 1961, p. 120.)

[3] John le Carré, *Smiley's People* (New York: Knopf, 1980), pp. 40, 277.

[4] Ibid., p. 152. Smiley's world is extended in le Carré, *A Perfect Spy* (1986). The radicalism of le Carré's fiction becomes clear by contrasting Smiley's eagerness to return to duty with David Webb's reluctance in Robert Ludlum's *The Bourne Supremacy* (1986). Before Webb changed his identity to Jason Bourne, he had been *happily* submerged in the routines of a married professor of Oriental studies in a New England college. He rejoins his old agency only after it manipulates him by having his wife abducted and playing on his sentiments to rescue her. Only then does Webb re-enter that morally indeterminate public life in which the minutest of occurrences (his turning down the thermostat of his house before leaving it) is meaning-saturated, in which survival depends on total alertness. Near the end of Ludlum's novel, Webb's wife says, "We all have a dark side, David. We wish we could deny it, but we can't. It's there. Perhaps we can't exist without it. Yours is a legend called Jason Bourne, but that's all it is." Webb answers saying that he loathes this dark side in which he

weary hero of *The Spy Who Came in from the Cold* (1964), lacks all principle and thus baffles his principled East German Communist interrogator. In or out of the cold, Leamas remains an actor who is altogether uncertain of the cause in which he might be enlisted. In a world of hypocrisy, betrayal, and lies, it does not matter what part he plays, whose side he's on. Deception surrounds him. He lives in a capricious, broken world—an unmapped gulag—in which all ideals have been discarded or betrayed. Everything demanded by his superiors—members of "the circus"—is unreal. Only his unceasing vigilance and talent for improvisation can keep the game of deceit and espionage a going concern.

For le Carré's hero there is no center—no authority other than "his own reason, his own humanity." To decide on a course of action, he must rely on what he himself has come to know. He is as reflective—as generous in his reflections—as he can manage in the specific situations in which he finds himself. His composed, meticulously observant mind records the remotest of sounds. Controlled by others, he yet controls himself. To him and his governmental agency, *everything* matters, which is to say that no particulars dominate. He is the thoroughgoing pragmatist whose affections and relationships are irrevocably contingent. Like the Buddha, he feels the tremors of the world, the pains of others. *He takes care.* And infinitely careful, he is—like God—dreadfully alone.

GRAHAM GREENE, TOO, keeps his agents, comedians, and travelers detached from transcending ideals. "I only know that he who forms a tie is lost. The germ of corruption has entered into his soul." Greene's *Human Factor* (1978) takes this epigraph from Joseph Conrad. To form ties is to come in from the cold, to become "sincere"; it is to confess truly, to tell the whole truth and nothing but the truth, to live without concealing anything, to stop wearing masks, to stop acting. The unheroic heroes of what Greene calls his "entertainments" doubt everyone's origins and present business. They treat everything as unsettled, indeterminate, unreal. They

---

had manifested himself as an actor. It was but an instrumental good which, as his wife remarks, brought them back together, and "that's all that matters." On the other hand, George Smiley has no affection for the private world which David Webb was forced to leave and to which Jason Borune happily returned.

take nothing for granted—not themselves, not the bureaucrats who brief them, not nature, not history, not God.

Living nowhere, such characters lead the way into a post-mythological space which we share whenever we recognize that behind the scenes, behind proclaimed victories, behind the politician's pretense of sincerity there are but further intrigues. In the process of demythologizing the structures that secure our lives we come to value only the intricacy of our demythologizing practices—the elaborate maneuvers of the all-seeing spy.[5] All that finally remains in this process is the will to enhance consciousness, to see the world clearly, to make it transparent. What we value, even if only in our fantasies, is the comprehensive voyeurism of the spy who, loyal only to his vocation of espionage, is determined to surmount the realities which confine him.

Infinitely attentive, alert to whatever he encounters, de-moralized and hollowed out, the idealized spy may yet be perceived as composed in the midst of a world so indubitably real that it is beyond mending. In the face of disintegration he discloses the *discipline* that controls the artistic process; he reveals that near the collapse of all he's shored up and remembered, near the end of all that's sensible and familiar, he possesses an acute spaced-out awareness of a present which includes the past and the future. For him, each moment is self-sufficient. He moves along with whatever befalls him; no course of action wastes his time. Disengaged, he looks around idly. This clairvoyant, omniscient voyeur is like the God of the

---

[5] My colleague Roger Hadlich has collected English words related to the Latin root *spec-*, which meant "look," "observe, and "appear." He has reminded me that a "speculum" is both a mirror in an optical instrument and a medical instrument for looking at things; that "specious" once meant simply good looking; that to "specify" (which contains a form of the Latin root "fact" ("to make") once meant to establish to what species something belonged; that we speak of "spectres," "spectacles," "spectators," and "spectaculars"; that—to return to le Carré's fiction—"spy" and "espionage" come to English through French from the Indo-European *spek-*, which relates to the modern English "skeptic" and the Greek "skopos," who is one who watches and from which we get the English "episcopalian," who (thanks to the addition of *epi*) watches "over" or "from above"; that "skopos" leads us to speak casually of telescopes and microscopes and less casually of scopophilia, which *Webster's Third International Dictionary* defines as "a desire to look at sexually stimulating scenes, esp. as a substitute for actual sexual participation." And so forth.

Renaissance to whom Jackson Cope's scholarship has called attention, a God who is "omnivoyant," the "sum total of each viewpoint, of every viewpoint," a God who knows Himself "through seeing and being seen—as spectator and spectacle, as audience and actor at once."[6]

Easily slipping past border guards, he crosses personal and national boundaries. Every fortified entity—his own ego, the implicit subject of his sentences—ceases to make a difference. He feels elated. It is a good day to live and, in the spirit of American Indians entering battle, a good day to die. He carries the weight of his past with the sovereign ease of the experienced actor who plays conflicting roles at will. For him all the world's a stage, a cabaret, a circus, a *play* of forces. At once player and playwright, he acts in territory between conflicting cultures and genres. At home nowhere but in this shadowless clearing, he plays—that is, he combines the real and the imagined, the past and the future in patterns in which contradictions become life-enhancing provocations. He is Jorge Luis Borges's Shakespeare who realized the meaning of being everyone and no one:

> There was no one in him; behind his face (which even in the poor paintings of the period is unlike any other) and his words, which were copious, imaginative, and emotional, there was nothing but a little chill, a dream not dreamed by anyone. . . .
>
> The story goes that, before or after he died, he found himself before God and he said: "I, who have been so many men in vain, want to be one man: myself." The voice of God replied from a whirlwind: "Neither am I one self; I dreamed the world as you dreamed your work, my Shakespeare, and among the shapes of my dream are you, who, like me, are many persons—and none."[7]

THE CHILL AT the actor's center—the intense eerie stillness of the spinning gyroscope—leaves no trace of itself. At her center there is but what she failed to eliminate—the cold ashes of all those parts she had seized to make herself distinctive and worthy, to make herself seem real. At best her

---

[6] Jackson I. Cope, *The Theater and the Dream: From Metaphor to Form in Renaissance Drama* (Baltimore: Johns Hopkins University Press, 1973), pp. 19, 100.

[7] Jorge Luis Borges, *Dreamtigers,* trans. Mildred Boyer and Harold Morland (Austin: University of Texas Press, 1964), pp. 46–47.

every impulse to distinguish and define, to focus and particularize, will have been integrated in her continuous spinning, her relating to whatever knot may make itself known. Resolved to keep play from coming to a dead end, she strives to outwit every intimation of death even as she courts it. She seeks not some climax or culmination but the inclusion of strange outsiders, of repressed impulses within herself. Only Death as ultimate Other remains critical—the constant critic of her action, an always-present stimulant that alerts her to her need for play to save herself.

In this view, play as well as politics must be a verb—a process of composing publicly whatever remains private and discrete. Being in action, having no footing and seeking none, those engaged in politics know themselves to be composed. Theirs is the serenity attributed to the Indian chief who in Thomas Berger's *Little Big Man* has just seen the tents of his tribe in flames, who knows his people to have no future, who remains light in his heaviness and allows his laughter to release what tension remains. For him, Death is a process in which dying is living and living is dying. Because he is reconciled to the end of history and therefore no longer directed by it, he is at play. He has "peaked" or, which comes to the same thing, "bottomed out." He has engaged in the kind of climb to the summit which David Roberts has remembered.

> Nothing stirred, only we lived; even the wind had forgotten us. Had we been able to hear a bird calling from some pine-tree, or sheep bleating in some valley, the summit stillness would have been familiar; now it was different, perfect. It was as if the world had held its breath for us. Yet we were so tired. . . . There was so little to do, nothing we really had the energy for, no gesture appropriate to what we felt we had accomplished: only a numb happiness, almost a languor. We photographed each other and the views, trying even as we took the pictures to impress the sight on our memories more indelibly than the cameras could on the film. . . . Trying to talk about it now would have seemed profane; if there was anything we shared, it was the sudden sense of quiet and rest.[8]

Roberts and his companions have peaked in full consciousness after the ground under them has given way. Without footholds or reference points, such actors line up to ride Disneyland's enclosed roller coaster in

[8] David Roberts, *The Mountain of My Feat* (New York: Vanguard Press, 1968).

the dark. Unable to anticipate the turns, steeled for all emergencies, they live in an ongoing state of emergency, an unrelieved crisis. As they play the role of screaming victims, they may shoot rapids in a canoe, oppose a father's demands, or rise to speak in a public meeting. Traveling in uncharted territory, they opt for acrophobia and stagefright, for access to terror. Knowing that anything can befall them, they have decided to surrender. Accepting the groundlessness of their maneuvers, they will sound out, engage, and adapt to the so-called realities they encounter. Women will present themselves as victims, children as schizophrenics, patriots as terrorists, Jews as Shylocks, artists as caterers to the status quo. The enhanced memory of these survivors impels them to treat the world as unreal. Their sensibility is that of survivors of Hiroshima who, carrying the past in their bones, will count on nothing and regard everything as contingent. To the extent that they keep recalling and commemorating their past, they are active in an aesthetic space, that is, in a groundless world where they construct their lives within the limits of an ungovernable reality.[9] For them, things are unambiguously what they are—unmediated, unsymbolized, desublimated. *All* symbols have been actualized, incarnated, realized. Word has been made flesh; the mind has become objective. Whatever distictions remain—the highs or lows of their experience—they are precisely those they designate, those they enact. For them there can *be* no objective crisis, surprise, emergency, accident. For them events are but designs, conceptulaizations imposed on an unbounded continuum within which everything flows except capitalized notions of Normalcy and Health, of Self and Others, of Life and Death. For them death can never be tragic or just or accidental. It's nothing in particular—merely how it goes.

Thus the victims of atomic bombardment, as Robert Lifton has noted, make no distinction between their victimizers and themselves. Such

---

[9] See Terrence Des Pres, *The Survivor: An Anatomy of Life in the Death Camps* (New York: Oxford University Press, 1976). The characters of Patricia Highsmith's thillers—Alfred Hitchock made her *Stranger on a Train* the best known—use the most familiar of conventional settings in which to display the consciousness of survivors. Traversing the streets of New York City, Highsmith's protagonists are exposed to ordinary and yet unpredictable events. They perceive everything, including themselves, in a spirit of uncanny neutrality. Insignificant objects put them on guard, silences alert them, objects "found in the street" (the title of her 1987 novel) make them apprehensive.

survivors feel "the power to make everything into nothing." Having "experienced a *permanent* encounter with death,"[10] they can identify nothing whatever that might have called for their experience, nothing that might bestow meaning on it and make it "appropriate." Their experience is the very essence of disproportionateness. They know something so totally incongruous that, quite simply, it cannot *be*. It is, so to speak, unreal. Whatever happened to them makes no sense. What residue of sense remains, it must be their construction, their own desperate make-belief. Having survived, having kept their balance, they act at will to create suitable, appropriate realities. At every moment they are new-born. Filled with knowledge, they seem naive.

Aleksandr Solzhenitsyn's "experiments" and "investigations" (as he has called his narratives) may make this sensibility more convincing. He has maintained that the inmates of the Gulag's camps—guards as well as prisoners—were permanently imprinted with a consciousness of death. They were made aware of the radical contingency of life, of the utter impossibility of assuming that anything necessarily determined anything else—that prudence is as little related to survival as recklessness. Arrests were for no definable offense; interrogations were endlessly about nothing; the terror was its own excuse for being. Solzhenitsyn remembers the prisoners' knowledge of death to be "the most basic, the steadiest form of Archipelago output there is—with no norms. . . . It was an accepted saying that *everything is possible* in Gulag. The blackest foulness and twist and turn of betrayal, the wildly unexpected encounters, love on the edge of the precipice. . . . " The great myth of Marxism failed to hold out hope: "Everything is steeped in lies, and *everybody knows it.*" And to be released from the camps was to move into a society unprepared for the survivor's easy acceptance of the all-devouring state: "If we get a letter completely free from self-pity, genuinely optimistic, it can only be from a former zek. They are used to the worst the world can do, and nothing can depress them."[11]

---

[10] In *The End of History* (1984) Barry Cooper refers to Robert J. Lifton, *Death in Life: Survivors of Hiroshima* (New York: Random House, 1967), pp. 541, 79 (my emphasis).

[11] Aleksandr I. Solzhenitsyn, *The Gulag Archipelago, 1918–1956: An Experiment in Literary Investigation* (New York: Harper & Row, 1973, 1975, 1976), vol. 2, pp. 221, 478; *Letter to the Soviet Leaders* (New York: Harper & Row, 1975), p. 62; *Gulag*, vol. 3, p. 462.

To be sure, such ungroundedness, such lightness of being, makes us deeply uneasy. We find it easier to be impressed by the firm moral commitment of Dr. Adelaide Hautval, a French concentration camp inmate who was ordered to participate in medical "experiments." As others have remembered, she said that "the only thing left to us is to behave for the short time that remains to us as human beings." Yet what norm of "human beings" is available to justify her courageous conduct? What standard transcends the technical, bureaucratic totality that led to her death? Unlike the survivors depicted by Solzhenitsyn, we can scarcely share a state of indifference, scarcely become "used to the worst the world can do."

And yet even as we honor our commitments to a transcendent morality, movies as conventional as Richard Rush's *Stunt Man* (1980) question it by allowing the hero to lose the support of moral foundations and emerge as quintessential actor. Having excaped the horrors of war and the terrors of holocausts in which nothing can be anticipated, such a hero strikes us as inexplicably composed.[12] Still, there are moments when, wholly open and totally lucid, we too emerge as gods shamelessly at play. At such moments we redesign the languages, myths, and rituals which fail us. Our play becomes inclusive; it absorbs highs and lows, past and future in an eternal presence. There is no Otherness independent of what we ourselves enact. We live in full consciousness and reach for no autonomous structure to bear up—no landmarks, no milestones, no frames. We enact as much reality as we can.[13] Our password becomes the slogan scrawled on Paris walls in 1968: "L'imagination au pouvoir." And our

---

[12] Compare Avigdor Arikha's practice of rushing to complete his canvases and sketches in at most a day and eschewing all retouching. Unfinished, they are complete. Having survived the Nazi terror in Rumania would seem to have conditioned him to invest fully in the moment. His works combine the finality and contingency, the discipline and the spontaneity displayed by the Zen masters of Chinese calligraphy.

[13] "Somehow the realization that nothing was to be hoped for had a salutary effect upon me," Henry Miller has written. "Walking toward Montparnasse I decided to let myself drift with the tide, to make not the least resistance to fate, no matter in what form it presented itself. . . . I made up my mind that I would hold on to nothing, that I would expect nothing, that henceforth I would live as an animal, a beast of prey, a plunderer. Even if war were declared, and it were my lot to go, I would grab the bayonet and plunge it, plunge it up to the hilt. And if rape were the order of the day then rape I would, and with a vengeance. . . . If to live is the paramount thing, then I will live, even if I must become a cannibal." (Henry Miller, *Tropic of Cancer* [New York: Grove Press, 1961], pp. 89–90.)

imagination is powerful insofar as it renames our cities, changes our masks, and reverses our roles within a state of permanent revolution, a timeless high noon in which nothing lasts long enough to cast its shadow. We are as innocent as infants before the fall; the terror we survived has informed us of our nakedness. We inhabit that world of unbridled social subjectivity which Jacques Derrida expressed as a commitment to "absolute chance" and "genetic indetermination."[14] We are the Kabbalists who, having survived the expulsion of the Jews from Spain, opposed the constraints of Talmudic scholarship and designed a strategy of interpreting sacred texts as well as their own lives in reference to a wholly arbitrary grid based on the numerical value of letters.[15] Thus whatever our text—whether it's a school, marriage, office, or hospital—we may yet capture moments for displacing its meaning by using it as pretext for enriching our lives. We may yet reject every ground for holding that any particular scripture must remain holy.

If such ground-breaking action defies nihilism this is because of the extent of its circularity. The Kabbalists' convoluted exercises end nowhere: they are the most indirect of trips toward the lightness of unidentified being—the direct one having become venerable, sanctimonious, and uninspiring. Elaborate detours they anticipate Derrida's kyphotic discourse, his deliberate effort to circumvent deadening institutions—specifically the canonized literature of graduate education (which Derrida had somehow survived) and to escape (as he has noted in a remarkably revealing aside) the German extermination camps.[16] All such practices aim at extending controlled experience. They aim at realizing what Roland Barthes called "the *pleasure* of the text," of participating in the spirited play of drifting metaphors, of remaining in an immaterial and unpredictable dance of meaning.

It is precisely action related to imagined limits which we assume to be real that intensifies the pleasure we take in our activities. The fiction

---

[14] Jacques Derrida, *Writing and Difference* (Chicago: University of Chicago Press, 1978), p. 292.

[15] See Gershom Scholem, *Kabbalah* (New York: New American Library, 1974), p. 337.

[16] See Derrida's essays in *Writing and Difference* (1978), commenting on Edmond Jabes's poem which recounts the story of two Holocaust victims.

that death is for real, that all the world's *not* a stage, surely intensifies one's performance. Thus actors become more intensively aware of themselves when they recall that beyond the stage there are screen tests and auditions, curtains and exits—not to mention critics and censors who destroy careers.

Such mindfulness of the limits we design for play is in any case integral to playfulness, and this notwithstanding talk about how players are "into it." The pleasure of play—the pleasure of the text—is the pleasure we take in being mindfully detached, in renouncing the unmediated, unplayed claims of experience. At play, we know ourselves *not* to yield to experience even as we are drawn toward losing self-consciousness. Our mindfulness keeps checking the impulse to end—agonizing us all the more when the boundaries fade and play is at its most precarious, when in extremis we are reaching the limits of consciousness. Thus our pleasure does not inhere in any specific class of activities but rather in our sheer awareness of our power to remain lucid while engaging the potent shadows surrounding us. The point is made in different terms by the Russian psychologist L. S. Vygotsky:

> Play continually creates demands on the child to act against immediate impulse. At every step the child is faced with a conflict between the rules of the game and what he would do if he could suddenly act spontaneously. In the game he acts counter to the way he wants to act. *A child's greatest self-control occurs in play.* He achieves the maximum display of willpower when he renounces an immediate attraction in the game (such as candy, which by the rules of the game he is forbidden to eat because it represents something inedible). Ordinarily a child experiences subordination to a rule and renunciation of action on immediate impulse as the means to maximize pleasure.[17]

How readily the means to which Vygotsky refers emerge as the end—as pleasure—becomes clear in the fluid politics of revolution when, at its highest pitch, people are inclusively and consciously in action—in a state of ecstasy which, as it sadly turns out, it is beyond their power to sustain. In such a state new roles, languages, and myths break established customs.

---

[17] L. S. Vygotsky, *Mind in Society: The Development of Higher Psychological Processes* (Cambridge: Harvard University Press, 1978), p. 99 (my emphasis).

The public arena is flooded by individuals who had not been visible before. Paupers, workers, prisoners, women, lunatics, and students enter public space and begin to see one another, to see themselves, to smile, laugh, and speak out. They are "possessed by a frenzied eloquence," as Flaubert recalled the Revolution of 1848.[18] Yet their frenzy is structured: they improvise scenes, dress up, express their mutual concerns, and, above all, talk loosely, the words pouring out.

Mikhail Bakunin was to recollect the days and nights of the Revolution as times of passionate involvement:

> Not only I but everyone was intoxicated: some from reckless fear, others from reckless rapture, from reckless hopes. I got up at five or even four in the morning and went to bed at two. I was on my feet all day, participated vigorously in all the meetings, gatherings, clubs, processions, outings, demonstrations; in a word, I imbibed with all my senses, through all my pores, the ecstatic atmosphere of revolution. It was a feast without beginning and without end.[19]

It is a time before virtue is defined, revolutionaries are decorated, and ranks are closed. It is the moment participants, aware of the newly made drama of their lives, simultaneously feel liberated and confirm their liberation. They know themselves to partake in an exalting spectacle, calling it a carnival, a festival, a masquerade. Theirs is no mere delirium but a conscious relating to their past and imagining of their future, a play in which they *constitute* a new world, each instant a completed, timeless achievement—what the actors later recall nostalgically as a time of pure joyousness.

And yet in the very midst of revolution is that poignant awareness of its death, a realization of limits which Benjamin Constance observed in the crowds he had witnessed in Paris in the 1790s:

> If during the outbreak of even that best prepared upheaval, you watch carefully the obscure ranks of the blind and subjugated populace, you will see that the people (even as it follows its leaders) casts its glance ahead to the

---

[18] Gustave Flaubert, *L'Education Sentimentale* (Paris: Editions Barnier Frères, 1964), p. 287.

[19] Mikhail Bakunin, *The Confessions of Bakunin* (Ithaca: Cornell University Press, 1977), p. 56.

> moment when these leaders will fall. And you will discern within its artificial exaltation, a strong combination of analysis and mockery. People will seem to distrust their own convictions. They will try to delude themselves by their own acclamations and to reinvigorate themselves by jaunty raillery. They foresee, so to speak, the moment when the glamour of it all will pass.[20]

This looking forward while still awed by the weight of the Old Order imparts to the crowds that extraordinary lucidity which is characteristic of the mountaineer who ascends a sheer wall:

> The climber's ongoing task is to tread the precarious ground between too much force and material, which leaves victory meaningless, and too little support and gear, which renders climbing impossible. A slip to one side may result in censure from one's climbing companions and peers, accusations of ethical transgression. A slip to the other way may leave the climber facing failure or even peril. Mountaineering is the process of overcoming physical obstacles but only when done within a carefully constructed and maintained normative framework. Mountaineering takes place on precarious ground, but it is often ground of the climbers' own choosing, rendered difficult and narrow by the rules they apply to themselves and others.
>
> As one mountain adventure follows another, recall and anticipation of mountain experience blend together. The individual is caught up in new patterns of relationships, finds new ways of judging self and others. Through these relationships mountaineers develop images of themselves as climbers, performing a role that is special and apart from conventional ones.[21]

THE MOUNTAINEER'S ACUTE ecological awareness is universalized in revolution. For its participants the whole world becomes sheer: nothing behind appearances matters. Nothing is there but transparency—and, of

---

[20] Quoted in Stephen Holmes, *Benjamin Constance and the Making of Modern Liberalism* (New Haven: Yale University Press, 1985).

[21] Richard G. Mitchell, Jr., *Mountain Experience* (Chicago: University of Chicago Press, 1984), p. 77.

course, whatever human beings, supported only by reflecting on one another's differences, have managed to install.

That such transparency defines modern times became clear to Nietzsche in the nineteenth century when he foresaw experiences which a later generation barely survived—those catastrophic historical developments that Hannah Arendt recalled after the Second World War. She affirmed that survivors who could bear to remember the time of their ordeal could no longer accept any a priori, God-given code for human action. For them, nothing is given but men's disposition for action itself. And being nothing but performers—however else human beings are said to appear—they are compelled, as Arendt was to say, "not only to find and devise new laws, but to find and devise their very measure, the yardstick of good and evil, the principle of their source." Like Nietzsche, Arendt was far from dismayed by this prospect. For her this meant "not the end of history but its first consciously planned beginning."[22] Ready to *make* history after its course had proved to be catastrophic, human beings are free to enrich their collective existence. In her essay on Bertolt Brecht, Arendt intimated how the nihilism of World War I and the technology of nuclear war and the death camps constituted nothing less than an opportunity for renewal. She envisaged Brecht as a young man wandering through Germany after the horror of the war:

> As it appeared to Brecht, four years of destruction had wiped the world clean, the storms having swept along with them all human traces, everything one could hold on to, including cultural objects and moral values. . . . It was as though, fleetingly, the world had become as innocent and fresh as it was on the day of creation. . . . Hence it was life that the young poet fell in love with—everything that the earth, in its sheer thereness, had to offer.[23]

And to engage in transactions with whatever appeared within this sheer thereness, it was necessary, Arendt argued, to enter that public arena which Aristotle had reserved for an autotelic, open-ended process of

---

22 Hannah Arendt, *The Origins of Totalitarianism* (New York: Harcourt, Brace, 1951), pp. 434–36 (my emphasis).

23 Hannah Arendt, *Men in Dark Times* (New York: Harcourt Brace & World, 1968), p. 229.

politics. Human beings implicated in this process aspire not to live up to an idealized transcendent reality but to keep creating reality. Quoting Aristotle, Arendt identified this arena as

> the space of appearance in the widest sense of the word, namely, the space where I appear to others as others appear to me, where men exist not merely like other living or inanimate things but make their appearance explicitly. . . . To be deprived of it means to be deprived of reality, which, humanly and politically speaking, is the same as appearance. To men the reality of the world is guaranteed by the presence of others, by its appearing to all; "for what appears to all, this we call Being" and whatever lacks this appearance comes and passes away like a dream, intimately and exclusively our own but without reality.[24]

In this formulation, the distinction between variable appearances and some ultimate Being is gone. The reality behind appearances only appears to be real: as human beings, we know only appearances and their infinite reflections. The shadows on the wall of the cave are but shadows of shadows cast by a sun projected to Plato's Socrates. The point of all our aspiring—our ultimate telos—is nothing definitive. It is derived from no underlying "real" foundation. Our end is but the fullest possible experience we bring to mind in an endless process in which we do no more than *make* appearances. At best, at our most human, we connect the disconnected events of our lives by participating in an interminable process in which we see ourselves sharing in the interplay of all phenomena. Within this process we necessarily retreat from anything final—any ideal—that has emerged independent of our performances. We reject appeals to some unchanging principle which presumes to justify excluding anyone from public life, which would disqualify mystics, fools, poets, children, women, or madmen. Nothing is diqualified by virtue of some unchanging a priori category; everything is regarded as potentially free to move within the time and space cleared for the realization of unrealized interests. There is no irrevocable rhyme or reason for drawing irrevocable lines between good and evil, means and ends, private and public, physician and patient,

---

[24] Hannah Arendt, *The Human Condition* (Chicago: University of Chicago Press, 1958), pp. 198–99.

garden and desert, life and death. We ourselves not only devise our own laws but (to repeat Arendt's words) "devise their very measure, the yardstick of good and evil, the principle of their source." Socially enacted laws alone organize our affairs. We ourselves are responsible for our past and our future, for opening and closing public arenas, for postulating points of entry and exit, birth and death.

Once existing boundaries are seen to be human enactments, the most basic of distinctions become precarious. The terms "self" and "environment" lose their conventional meaning: they cease to be regarded as objectively circumscribed, as some independent domain *out* there. Outside and inside, background and foreground, center and margin emerge as concepts which become deadening fixations once separated from our reality-making activity, from our acts of focusing, identifying, and defining. To fragment the flux of experience, and to allow the fragments to become fixed, is to submit to the autonomy of familiar polarized distinctions:

heaviness – lightness
defense – offense
necessity – freedom
reality – appearance
private – public
involvement – detachment

When such concepts lose their fixed boundaries, excluded interests make their appearance. Assuming the form of frightening and exhilarating revolutionary movements, they displace secure centers of power. In a context that betrays his ambivalence, George Kateb has identified the basic aim of such movements:

> The aim is to rehabilitate the idea of citizenship and to extend the practice of citizenship into as many areas of life as possible; from the original locus of citizenship, i.e., public affairs, to private institutions and associations and activities of almost every sort. What is in play is a positive concept of politics, and a corresponding desire to make as many kinds of human relations as possible into political relations. Put negatively, there is a disdain for passivity. There is a repugnance toward being administered,

> commanded, or manipulated; and beyond that, a repugnance toward being represented. The perversions of "usual politics" are not the only object of attack: usual politics itself stands under indictment. The spokesmen for participation want, insist on, politics; want it for themselves and for others; seek to extend it as far as it can be extended, until tiredness sets in. But it is politics without hierarchy, procedures, delimited purposes, legalism, practiced compromise, and permanent roles, as well as politics without *frozen* postures, fakery, cheating, arrogance, self-imposition, and rivalry. It is politics as conversation, not speeches; transaction, not battle.[25]

It is a politics which at its best creates and transforms its own hierarchies, procedures, and legalisms, its own rules for maintaining one's balance in a world in which crisis and emergency are not discrete moments but a universal condition, not specific problems to be solved but the very nature of existence.

Burdened by this condition we understandably yearn for some stabilizing orientation. We come to share that mute nostalgia displayed by Madame Raphael, one of Milan Kundera's characters in *The Book of Laughter and Forgetting* (1981). A teacher who joined group after group in quest of salvation, she finally hoped to be wholly united with her students and form "a single body and a single soul, a single ring and a single dance." Once she roamed the streets of the small French Riviera town of her school and reached for primal ground: "Suddenly she raised her head as if sensing a sliver of melody on the wings of a breeze, a fragrance from far-off lands. She stopped and in the depths of her soul heard the rebellious scream of a void yearning to be filled. She felt that somewhere nearby a flame of great laughter was flickering and perhaps somewhere not far off a group of people was holding hands and dancing in a ring."[26]

YEARNING FOR COMPLETION, we may yet be able to follow Samuel Beckett's Molloy, who waiting and waiting at the edge of nausea, manages

---

[25] George Kateb, in J. Roland Pennock and John W. Chapman, eds., *Participation in Politics* (New York: Lieber-Atnerton, 1975), p. 91 (my emphasis).

[26] Milan Kundera, *The Book of Laughter and Forgetting* (New York: Knopf, 1981), p. 65.

to control himself by transferring sixteen "sucking stones" from pocket to pocket. Confronting the end, we can still divert ourselves, lose interest in true foundations, and thereby allow for the emergence of that comprehensive aestheticism which Alvin Gouldner, calling it a dramaturgic perspective, has seen as characteristic of times when historical events are so inexplicable that they make us reflective—as they made an elite of Athenians reflective in the third century B.C. Gouldner recalled that at such times a Plato enters, writes scenarios, inspires actors, and engenders dialogues:

> The dramaturgic view of life arises when experience is losing its continuity and is dissolving into episodic shreds, when the larger architecture of experience is crumbling, when the rhythm and movement of life sprawls and lacks organizing centers or familiar punctuations and accents. The dramaturgic view arises when living leaves no sense of residual accomplishment, where each moment is much like the other (for there are no culminations in prospect), and when men are becoming dangerously bored. It is when social theorists do not believe that "the best is yet to come," when they lose a sustaining sense of the upward trend, that they devise dramaturgic perspectives on human life and groups. A Plato enters, then, when social theorists come to feel that history has no exit.
>
> Such dramaturgy has its inner dialectic. On the one side, it insists on the importance of appearances, for it says that appearances are normally all we have and may therefore constrain us to take them seriously. On the other side, the dramaturgic view devalues realms of life that men ordinarily imbue with special value, for it tells us that, like the others, they, too, are no more than appearances. In saying that appearances count and that how things look is important, the dramaturgic view says that life is serious. Yet it *is* appearance—a flickering shadow on the wall of the cave—and should not be taken too seriously. This ambivalence about the seriousness with which life may be viewed is expressed quite clearly in Plato: "[H]uman afairs are hardly worth considering in earnest and yet we must be in earnest about them—a sad necessity constrains us."
>
> The dramaturgic view heightens an appreciation of things conventionally slighted and slights things conventionally exalted. . . .
>
> There is, of course, one way in which Plato seems to have set himself apart from and against a dramaturgic view of life, for the latter implies that

> there is no significant difference between the world and the stage, or between visible, mere appearances and a hidden, truer reality, while Plato's theory of the Forms asserts the very opposite. But in the end the two converge, for Plato's insistence on the reality of the Forms maintains the distinction between appearance and reality only by removing reality from life as men experience it. It thus leaves the world—as the dramaturgists did and do—as a sphere where the distinction fades and all is now appearances.[27]

And it is in this world that we are unconditionally at play even as we create illusions which reject this, even as exiled from the Garden of Eden we arm ourselves with an array of mythologies, metaphors, and organizations so as to master some Nature "out there," even as (reading Plato as if he were a Platonist) we presume to leave the cave and dream of coming in touch with a reality that will provide the laws that assure our salvation.

While there is no denying this potent and perhaps irrevocable dream, neither nature nor history pulls itself together to disclose nature's or history's regularities and patterns. When desolate and in dire need of consolation we can scarcely acknowledge this. Rather than admit the absence of the gods we will tell ourselves that they send their favorites to the death camps. Thus in his Jerusalem Journal, Melville wondered (as Nietzsche was to wonder later) if perhaps the Holy Land's desolate landscape was perhaps "the result of the fatal embrace of the Deity."[28]

Although the gods appear as an autonomous force so as to confirm humanity's designs, their sheer dynamism engenders no language which allows us to belief that our designs approximate their mandate. Should we claim to "discover" that E really does equal mc^2, should we find this more or less confirmed, the confirmation holds only at the precise moment we are looking—which, to be sure, may be good enough for us, good enough simply because it allows us to act *for the time being*. If in our process of inquiry we do arrive at this or that conclusion, this is not because the gods or nature or history told us it's true independent of our experimental

---

[27] Alvin W. Gouldner, *Enter Plato* (New York: Basic Books, 1965), pp. 386–87.

[28] Herman Melville, *Journal of a Visit to Europe and the Levant* (Princeton: Princeton University Press, 1955), p. 154.

action but rather because we found it in our present interest to make it true. After all, given the will we can push the moon off its allegedly natural course and, as the death camps taught both its victims and guards, we ourselves can deprive human beings of their allegedly natural behavior.

To accept nature as a wholly *in*definite presence which declines to make rules is to see a pebble as clearly as Roquentin saw it in the opening pages of Sartre's *Nausea*—as an irreducibly meaningless expanse that, *like everything else,* fits no categories. We become nauseated. Yet to hear nature speak the unambiguous language of a natural science is to surrender to its mandates and no less to lose control of ourselves. Unable to dismiss nature as legislator and too skeptical to accept its alleged laws, we can but vacillate. Near vertigo and nausea we can maintain our balance only by maneuvering between the heaviness and lightness of being.

5 THE UNGROUNDED POLITICS OF PLAY

TODAY, the oppositional projects of contemporary arts are near exhaustion: their integration in the movement of modernity keeps them from encompassing and transfiguring it. The realities produced by the economy and society of capitalism, its very museums, would seem to anticipate the artist's every twist. The products of technology are in position before the artist arrives with his sculptures, earthworks, scripts, installations, novels, and sounds. "Capitalism," Jean-Francois Lyotard has noted, "inherently possesses the power to derealize familiar objects, social roles, and institutions to such a degree that the so-called realistic representations can no longer evoke reality except as nostalgia or mockery."[1] Technology, what is more, breaks both the artist and the artistic process into fragments and uses the fragments to stimulate the market and thereby itself. Twenty years after its production, the Beatles' "Revolution" finds its way into commercials to sell shoes for Nike Corporation. The technological drift itself, as Paul Fussell concluded in his

---

[1] Jean-Francois Lyotard, *The Postmodern Condition* (Minneapolis: University of Minnesota Press, 1984), p. 74.

reflections on the literature of World War I, "domesticates the fantastic and normalizes the unspeakable."[2] Moreover, contemporary works of art are increasingly predesigned to enter preexisting markets. Duly merchandized, they are emblems of good taste, icons of wealth, representatives of the discourse of modernity. In the form of commodities they provide, in Robert Hughes's phrase, "the background hum for power."[3] Disinfected by both the schools and the mass media, domesticated by impeccable tour guides such as Alastair Cook, they are venerated as masterpieces and assimilated by the reigning culture. As Fredric Jameson has noted, they become auxiliaries of commerce and social intercourse:

> For one thing, commodity production and in particular our clothing, furniture, buildings and other artifacts are now intimately tied in with styling changes which derive from artistic experimentation; our advertising, for example, is fed by postmodernism in all the arts and inconceivable without it. For another, the classics of high modernism are now part of the so-called canon and are taught in schools and universities—which at once empties them of their older subversive power.[4]

To be sure, the imperium of technology is no seamless totality. If modernism is dated, the desperate stopgap ventures of postmodernist art continue to demonstrate the possibility of taking an independent stand. Consumable art objects continue to be replaced by unconsumable performance art, self-destructive sculpture, and ephemeral, useless enterprises

---

2 Paul Fussell, *The Great War and Modern Memory* (New York: Oxford University Press, 1975), p. 74.

3 Robert Hughes, *The Shock of the New* (New York: Knopf, 1981), p. 111. On the capitalist appropriation of art, see Serge Guilbaut, *How New York Stole the Idea of Modern Art* (Chicago: University of Chicago Press, 1983). Marxist regimes are no different in their impact on the arts. With heavy irony, Miklos Haraszti has noted that in socialist countries the relation between the state and the artist (especially in television, film, and theater) is so symbiotic that censorship and prohibition are dispensable. Opposition fades as the state has its way and the artist is free—freely and gratefully functioning within it. He is a functionary, a cog in "an all-embracing cultural mechanism whose attention is directed primarily inward to ensure that no one element disturbs the whole." (Miklos Haraszti, *The Velvet Prison: Artists under State Socialism* [New York: Basic Books, 1977], p. 112.)

4 Fredric Jameson, "Postmodernism and Consumer Society," in Hal Foster, ed., *The Anti-Aesthetic* (Port Townsend, Wash.: Bay Press, 1983), p. 124.

such as Christo's. Postmodernists persist in contradicting manifest reality by abandoning subject matter, by breaking the frames and pedestals of their structures. Nonetheless, they keep being defeated in their efforts to maintain their balance by swimming more energetically than the currents which carry them.[5] Yet to respect their obstinate refusal to provide end-products and their resolve to keep acting in the territory between certainties—to value their posture despite their defeats—is to give recognition to inconsequential maneuvers not only in the arts but wherever we might locate them.

Although noninstrumental action—a *mere* balancing of powers—is suppressed in contemporary art, science, and politics, it is in fact not unknown to us in other domains. If only in some nursery or on some playground, all of us have pursued activities we knew to be useless—good for nothing beyond themselves. Thus we can easily acknowledge infants at play to be innocent of any "higher" goals their play may serve. Whatever moralists or sociobiologists allege,[6] we don't see the movements of infants as efforts to satisfy socially or biologically defined objectives. Like holocaust survivors, infants are touched only by what they touch, by their immediate surroundings. Amoral opportunists, they are grounded not in history but in their own ever-changing practices. They improvise from scratch in the plenitude of undivided time and bottomless space. Slowly, carefully probing the world about them, they make and test distinctions. Always for the present moment, they treat some things as foreground and others as background, some as weighty and others as light.

Reflecting on children at play may enable us to accept what we tacitly know, for all of us once moved so as to dissolve and recapture whatever we impinged upon, whatever impinged on us. In this process we

---

[5] Jack Burnham has reviewed a series of postmodernist fiascos including exhibitions of "Cybernetic Serendipity" (Institute of Contemporary Arts, London, 1968), "Software" (Jewish Museum, New York, 1969), "Art and Technology" (Los Angeles County Museum, 1967–71), and the opening of the Center for Advanced Visual Studies at the Massachusetts Institute of Technology (1968). ("Art and Technology," in Kathleen Woodward, ed., *The Myths of Information* [London: Routledge & Kegan Paul, 1980].)

[6] For examples of empirical reductionism, see Brian Sutton-Smith, ed., *Play and Learning* (New York: Gardner Press, 1979), and Jerome S. Bruner et al., *Play: Its Role in Development and Behavior* (New York: Basic Books, 1976).

became progressively more competent, more able to control excitements of ours which interfered with our movement toward enlarging our scope of action. We kept balancing our need for structures with our need for displacing them. If we were attached to footholds, it was but to facilitate our departure from them. If we remained attached to retreats, it was but to catch our breath and prepare for new encounters. Yet though all this was useful—something done in order to do something more—its use was wholly generalized: it was useful for everything, that is, for nothing in particular. Thus our play had value beyond any specific lesson it ostensibly taught, any good it allegedly did. Unconstrained by anything but our own perceptions, wholly at play, we failed (as we were to say later) to be guided by some fixed moral code. We simply valued rules to the extent that they empowered us to come to terms with inexplicable Otherness. Freely changing the rhythms and boundaries of our activities, we taunted paternal guides who claimed to know the demands of reality.

Although we come of age in a culture that is systematically grounding the play of the arts along with the play of politics and science, we still tolerate the amoral playfulness of children. And remembering what it's like to play, we recognize play when we see it. Moving among untended children—the most obvious place to look for unadulterated play—we know they are playing when we perceive their sheer desire to keep it up, in fact to keep doing it past bedtime way into the night. Seeing them at play, we are led to question our belief in the supposedly necessary contradiction between work and play, seriousness and playfulness, pain and pleasure. For children at play these polarities seem to have fused. And as we sense their desire to keep it up, even their most strenuous and agonizing efforts will strike us as play. After all, no one is *making* them do it. Clearly, not even the most hard-working of players are *forced* to play. Their activity seems wholly to satisfy them. They're playful; they're absorbed. Playing G. I. Joe, cowboys and indians, cops and robbers, doctor-patient-nurse, enacting scenarios which express possibilities of experience, their behavior reveals the fullness, seriousness, and resoluteness of their reenactments of such previously enacted roles as astronaut, mother, shopkeeper, or bicycle racer. We feel (in a phrase that turns out to be misleading) that they're "into it." We know they're on a *play*ground by the way we as observers become apprehensive when one of their make-believe props threatens to become real—as when a child's wagon is out of control and threatens a *real* injury. We know what's happening: the spirit of their activity is about to be destroyed. As playtime and playspace disappear, the players—all actors—lose the chance to impersonate, improvise, pretend, act. When they lose control of their playground, their outcries become as uncontrolled as one's trembling with stagefright—one's anxiety that the stage ends where the unknown audience begins.[7] Something real—an uncontrolled reality—puts an end to play and acting. When children play—and when they cease to play—we know it as well as Thomas Beard, writing in 1631, knew the difference between appearance and reality, between what he called show and deed: "In a certain place there was acted a tragedie of the death and passion of Christ not in show but in deed . . . : for he that played Christ's part, hanging upon the Crosse, was wounded to death by him that should have thrust his sword into a bladder full of blood tied to his side."[8]

OUT OF HIS analysis of the world of childhood, psychiatrist D. W. Winnicott arrived at the view that the purest of all playgrounds is the space between the virtually egoless infant and the wholly supportive, nurturing mother.[9] This space, he said, is the arena in which action is

---

[7] "Stage fright," Clifford Geertz has said, "consists, of course, in the fear that, for want of skill or self-control, or perhaps by mere accident, an aesthetic illusion will not be maintained, that the actor will show through his part. Aesthetic distance collapses, the audience (and the actor) lose sight of Hamlet and gain it, uncomfortably for all concerned, of bumbling John Smith painfully miscast as the prince of Denmark. In Bali, the case is the same: what is feared is that the public performance to which one's cultural location commits one will be botched and that the personality—as we would call it but the Balinese, of course, not believing in such a thing, would not—of the individual will break through to dissolve his standardized public identity. When this occurs, as it sometimes does, the immediacy of the moment is felt with excruciating intensity and men become suddenly an unwillingly creature, locked in mutual embarrassment, as though they had happened upon each other's nakedness." (*Local Knowledge* [New York: Basic Books, 1983], p. 64.)

[8] Thomas Beard, *Theatre of God's Judgement* (1631), quoted in Anne Richter, *Shakespeare and the Idea of Play* (Westport, Conn.: Greenwood Press, 1962), p. 17.

[9] See D. W. Winnicott, *Playing and Reality* (London: Tavistock, 1971), and Sigmund Freud, "Construction in Analysis," in *Complete Psychological Works* (London: Hogarth, 1975), vol. 23, pp. 355–70.

uncoerced and unmanipulated. It is an approximation of the setting for psychoanalysis as well as for Jürgen Habermas's "ideal speech situation" within which meanings are constructed and tested.[10] Because nothing but the infant imposes meaning on whatever occurs in this arena, Winnicott saw it as *ground* for play, as its very condition. To the infant such neutral no-man's-land is but a meaningless, awesome expanse. When something occurs within it—say, his own fingers have moved involuntarily—the infant is free to *make* something of the occurrence, free to act. We assume his motion to be deliberate and purposeful, to be his own, for we cannot explain his repeating it by reference to some preexisting order of behavior. It's disorderly, not called for. It's unconditioned, hence not *knowable.* What is happening, we feel, is not altogether required, not simply natural. It's at least partially a groundless, gratuitous intimation of the capacity for doing the unexpected. What had appeared to be an involuntary movement was, when repeated, augmented *needlessly,* changed in direction of speed. And nothing, it seems to us, had called for such astonishing versatility—nothing, that is, except the infant's idle, disengaged "curiosity," his will to experiment, to determine what he might get away with. He makes his fingers move; he plays with them. Appropriating an occurrence, he is conscious of his action.

The neutral space within which he acts dictates no specific conduct: its emptiness allows him to distinguish his moving fingers, to *give* them boundaries. Having both time and space, he constructs a relationship which allows experience to appear in some *particular* way, some *distinc-*

---

[10] Distinguishing "genuine communication" from instrumental, utilitarian action, Habermas postulates an ideal which is so uncontaminated by instrumental action that it becomes, as Barbara Herrnstein-Smith has pointed out, sumblimely empty. The actual market in which communication takes place, she rightly objects, is never uncontaminated, never devoid of conflicting interests and economies, of nonsymmetrical powers. For her, Habermas endorses a "superlunary universe" which excludes the profit motive; it is one "where no wind blows ill and there need be no tallies of cost and benefit, where there are no exchanges but only gifts, where all debts are paid by unrepayable acts of forgiveness." She regards such communication not as politics but as an escape from politics. (Barbara Herrnstein-Smith, "Value without Truth-Value," unpublished paper elaborated in *Contingencies of Value: Post-Axiological Perspectives in Critical Theory* [Cambridge: Harvard University Press, forthcoming].)

tive time, some *specific* light. When he sees the event in the constraining terms of his expectation, illusion, dream, fantasy, projection, or hypothesis, it is no longer simply "out there." He has appropriated it. It has become known—brought into relief as a particular fact, as a discrete happening distinguished from happenings that precede or follow it, that are close or distant. It has been given form and significance. Having acted on the basis of a postulate—an imagined form—the infant, now the actor, becomes free from the grip of his experience. Having come to terms with it, he ceases to be "into it." He has managed to become detached from an occurrence which, because it had absorbed him, had limited his capacity for action. His playtime and playground allowed him to engage in a transaction with uncomprehended experience.

His "curiosity" is grounded in nothing more firm than the encouraging silence of his mother, of whoever promotes sheer virtuosity, sheer interest in making one's own scene, in acting on one's own. And *her* discipline consists of applauding her child's action without imposing standards provided by her familiar world. She supports purposeful action without endorsing any specific purpose.[11] To be sure, she may judge one or another of his acts to be unwise insofar as it diminishes his freedom to remain in action. But in relation to her child she knows no other morality. She may realize what is risked by her indiscriminate support—and yet bear the knowledge that she might be mistaken about what her child can bear at the moment. For him, she knows, life can well be too much: there are deadly waves beyond his play, and she may have failed to judge his power to cope with them. Thus his mother too is at play, for she is no less experimenting, no less risking failure—*their* failure.

The risky character of such performances became clear to Peter Marin, an educator who reported on an experiment conducted near the end of an elementary school class. The teacher asked her students to write whatever they wished without bothering about established rules and then to read back to one another whatever they had written. Marin reports, "So they stood in their various places and tried to make sense of what they

---

[11] "*Beauty,*" Immanuel Kant wrote in a much-quoted passage, "is the form of the purposiveness of an object, so far as this is perceived in it without an representation of purpose." (*Critique of Judgment*, trans. J. H. Bernard [New York: Hafner, 1951], p. 73.)

had done. No couplets. No moon and spoon. Instead, a batch of unreadable scrawls that were socially useless—for they could not be read aloud. Some began to cry, and others turned to me with betrayed and angry faces, for they had broken free and there was no way to express what they had done within the rituals of their given world." They had been encouraged to withdraw from inhibiting structures and enter that unobstructed, bottomless space where familiar rhymes and reasons ceased to govern. Languages and myths and rituals that normally bound them—their shared source of power—having been suspended, they found themselves, as Marin saw it, in that turbulence out of which myths are formed. Some of the students were crushed by their released primordial impulses while others pulled themselves together, confronted what they experienced, and determined to create new ways—new structures—for giving meaning to their lives. In either case they had been thrown into political space, a neutral zone for a living theater:

> "Social reality" dissolves around us into raw repression; we drift, disconnected in the country of demons and delights. There is nothing to ground or hold us, imagination reigns and we begin, haltingly, confusedly to live out our dreams. There is both a loveliness and a terror to that, for we seem to be flying and failing at the same time, moving through ourselves toward the raw stuff at the heart of being itself. . . . New myths can form only in the unmediated experience—in some kind of ragged, direct and brutal coupling. That is where we have been thrown by the slant of the times; in and down to confront in ourselves the sempervirid archetypes and demons and energies from which, with luck, we will make a new way of seeing and speaking.[12]

WE KEEP OUR apocalyptic impulses from dominating our lives when we engage in those games which Steward Culin, an early American ethnologist, saw as originating in magic rites of divination. When we fail to divine we cannot transform that deadly, nameless Otherness which rumbles beyond the range of those structures which check and balance our brute

---

[12] Peter Marin, "Tripping the Heavy Fantastic," *New York Times Book Review,* February 21, 1971, p. 7.

nature and its technological extension. Without playing games we cannot enact our lives—either our advances or our retreats. At the end of Crockett Johnson's popular children's book *Harold and the Purple Crayon* (1955), four-year-old Harold tired of his adventurous walk in the moonlight. To find his way back to his bedroom, he used his crayon to draw what he needed: he drew his bedroom window around the moon, found his bed, proceeded to get into it, and, crayon still in hand, drew up the covers. As he gladly fell asleep, his crayon dropped to the floor. Having *decided* to retreat—to lose the world—he lost the distance between himself and his experience; *deciding* he had gone far enough "Harold dropped off to sleep."

If our games can lead us to withdraw from excessive excitements, they can no less generate new excitements, release unaccepted impulses, encourage role-reversal, and expand our horizons. As we adopt new roles, meaningless routines are decentered. Tennis players who ponder Timothy Gallwey's *The Inner Game of Tennis* learn to arouse subdued aspects of their personalities by changing their styles of playing:

> After they have played tennis for a year or so, most people fall into a particular pattern of play from which they seldom depart. Some adopt a defensive style; they spare no effort to retrieve every ball, lob often, hit deep into the opponent's court, and seldom hit the ball hard or go for a winner. The defensive player waits for his opponent to make an error and wears him down by degrees with endless patience. Some Italian clay-court players are the prototype for this style.
>
> The opposite of this is the offensive style adopted by some great and would-be great American players. In its extreme form the ball is hit for a winner every time. Every serve is designed to be an ace, every return of serve a clean passing shot, while volleys and overheads are all aimed to land within one or two inches of the lines.
>
> A third common pattern is what might be called the "formal" style of play. Players in this category don't care so much where their ball goes as long as they look good stroking it. They would rather be seen using flawless form than winning the match.
>
> In contrast, there is the competitive style of the player who will do anything to win. He runs hard and hits hard or soft, depending on what seems to bother his opponent most, and used gamesmanship to the hilt.

> One final style worth mentioning is that of the detached Buddhist. He plays with perfect serenity, aware of everything but attached to nothing; that is, even though he makes great effort, he seems unconcerned with the results of his actions. Always alert, he shows no tension even on match point.
>
> Having outlined these basic styles to a group of players, I often suggest that as an experiment they adopt the style that seems most unlike the one they have previously adopted. I also suggest that they act the role of a good player, no matter what style they have chosen. Besides being a lot of fun, this kind of role-playing can greatly increase a player's range. The defensive player learns that he can hit winners; the aggressive one finds that he can also be stylish. I have found that when players break their habitual patterns, they can greatly extend the limits of their own style and explore subdued aspects of their personality.[13]

Roles and rules are changed to distance us, as Richard Sennet has observed, from ossified structures which put an end to play:

> A game of marbles is a competitive situation in which the aim is for one of the players to get all the marbles of the other players, or, under a different set of rules, to wipe the other players' marbles off the playing field. If the adult observer tries to simplify the rules of the game, he encounters resistance from the children. What they like are attempts to make the rules more and more complex. If the game were just a means to an end, their behavior would make no sense. *Acquisition is the reason children play, but not the play itself; the complication of the rules children favor instead delays the acquisitive end as long as possible. . . .*
>
> The tools which permit children to delay, to remain in a state of play, are the rules. A game of marbles is thus a complicated affair. It is only by erecting rules that the children keep themselves free of the outside, non-play world. The more complicated the rules are, the longer the children are free. . . .
>
> These rules are acts of self-distance for two reasons. The first is that mastery over others is put off. It is striking how angry children become

[13] W. Timothy Gallwey, *The Inner Game of Tennis* (New York: Random House, 1974), p. 62.

> when one person in a game of marbles is detected cheating. When one child tries to gain a more immediate dominance over the other children than he or she would have in sticking to the rules, the play seems spoiled for everybody. Thus the conventions of a child's game put the child's pleasure in dominating others at a distance, even though domination is the reason the game is played, even though domination is strongly desired throughout.
>
> The second way rules become acts of self-distance concerns the control of inequalities of skill among the players. Long-distance marbles, for example, is a game requiring good muscular coordination in order to shoot the marble straight. A child of four and a half is physically at a disadvantage here with a child of six. When small children are put with older children and asked to play long-distance marbles, the older children immediately decide to change the rules so that the little ones will not be instantly eliminated. The older children invent a "handicap" for themselves, to establish equality among the players, and thus prolong the game. Again the rules take the children away from direct assertion of themselves, from immediate mastery. Self-distance here too gives structure to play.[14]

Rules which have served to distance us at one time from oppressive structures may of course later turn out to become so binding that play all but collapses. Yet even if they cannot be broken, even if the rules and the rulers almost triumph and action appears as rule-bound behavior, it may still be possible to play in the midst of what has become reality. Without betraying ourselves by any overt act, we may yet play on what we alone treat as a stage, diverted from ending only by our imagination. We may then remain in touch with the dominant powers by articulating them, our language being our last resort for breaking them up. Still in action we can reflect on how ingeniously we are being diminished, how subtly we are being victimized, how cunningly the very playground we need to outwit reality is being extinguished. Intrigued by adverbs, we may remain active until forced into that extreme, strictly mindless state which is wholly consummating, which consumes us as actors.

Not to despair is to persist in designing structures that are more

---

[14] Richard Sennett, *The Fall of Public Man* (New York: Knopf, 1977), pp. 318–19 (emphasis supplied).

comprehensive than those which have become dull, banal, and finally deadening. It is to impose patterns on pure being and thereby to appropriate it. "The inventor of the Sabbath—call him Moses if you wish—declared the cycle of the earth null." Cynthia Ozick continues: "What do the birds, the worms their prey, the corn in the field, men and animals who sleep and wake up hungry, know of a Sabbath, this arbitrary call to make a stop in the diurnal rhythm, to move consciously apart from the natural progression of days?"[15] Whether the structures we design and impose are felt to be as changeable as the *frame* of the Sabbath, or as natural as the *rhythms* of the seasons, they nevertheless remain the very condition for continuous play. In their absence, there is no impetus to enact alternative realities for ourselves. However frustrating the fixed bars of a jungle gym, they give support to exuberant exercises. However frustrating the conventions of the limerick, they entice the poet to become imaginative. The ingenious provisions of the tax law, like the inexplicable demands of one's parents, provoke us to come up with novel interpretations of given codes. One's interpretation of parental instructions or of the Internal Revenue Code adds a measure of suspense to a world that is ungenerous in providing excitements and trials. Refinements and complications of rules induce us to invent new contexts for making vaguely felt discomforts comprehensible. To *say* that one's pains are "the cries and whispers of the flesh" is to place them in a larger frame. Thus a game Brian Sutton-Smith invented made it possible for his children to manage the troublesome contradictions of their lives:

> I sometimes pretend to be Frankenstein or the Werewolf and, baring my teeth, and lifting my arms stiffly, move in their direction. When I galumph in this manner, they laugh and run and I laugh. . . . Then on other occasions when they scold me or protest, I do the opposite. I exaggerate my abasement. I pretend to cry. I sob and sob, head bowed. Again we all laugh. . . . What I am doing besides playing, is saying that:

---

[15] Cynthia Ozick, *Five Fictions* (New York: Knopf, 1982), pp. 62–63. Georges Perec's *Life: A User's Manual* (1986) escapes the banality of familiar genres by arbitrarily dividing his work into one hundred narrative units that provide the setting of ten apartments in which he presents the most ordinary behavior of his compartmentalized characters so precisely that his account becomes comic.

> (a) I am your dangerous father.
> (b) But my exaggeration shows that it is under my control and so not unpredictably dangerous to you.
>
> And again:
>
> (a) I am your softhearted booby father.
> (b) But it is under my control and I am not a complete pushover.
>
> So once again I am making beliefs even while I am playing. I am saying to my children, all these contradictory feelings can continue to exist and this is how it can be done. The joy of playfulness may thus be the marvel and brilliance of our frame-making reconciliation of real-world ambiguities.[16]

Such make-belief allows contradictory feelings to exist side by side. It blocks the movement toward frenzy, toward the resolve to eliminate one side or the other. Keeping us from being hostage to unstructured feelings, it increases comprehension.[17]

As children gain in power, ingenuity, and skill, they rely on others and themselves to become conscious of an increasingly wider range of experience. Reorganizing the forces which organize their lives, they treat a stranger as friend, night as day, or dessert as dinner. Like Dostoyevsky's Underground Man, they change the most reasonable rule not because it is unreasonable but rather because it keeps life unchanged. And yet when rules have faded, when no pressure is felt and the world freely floods in, children take pains to invent structures with which to comprehend the flood of experience. Seeking to see the world whole, continuously balancing advances and retreats, they play.

---

[16] Sutton-Smith, *Play and Learning*, p. 319.

[17] "When we have had an experience," Hans-Georg Gadamer says, "this means that we possess it. We can now predict what was previously unexpected. The same thing cannot become again a new experience for us; only some other unexpected thing can provide someone who has experience with a new one. Thus the experiencing consciousness has reversed its direction, i.e., it has turned back on itself. The experiencer has become aware of his experience, he is experienced! He has acquired a new horizon within which something can become an experience for him." (*Truth and Method* [New York: Seabury Press, 1975], p. 317.)

WE REMAIN BALANCED by keeping the forces endangering us at a proper distance—proper because they are neither so close that they become nerve-wracking nor so far that they fail to stimulate. We are endangered by relentless excitation—a pleasurable itch becoming agonizing over time—as well as by an economy so monotonous that it fails to generate excitement. In either case, it is continuous sameness that drives us out of our minds. To vary our experience, we change familiar structures, patterns, grids, mazes, and networks. Changing them, we renew our perceptions, develop resources for acting, and keep on the move.

When structures function properly, they articulate—break up, deconstruct—the dead weight that bears down on us. They name, measure, and choreograph; they leave us less dumbfounded, less numbed, less brutalized. Suspending our deadlines, they divert us from finalities, from whatever we have come to categorize as ultimates—Nature, History, Necessity, Fate, or simply The Facts. When the forces of so-called reality cease to arouse us or else demand an excess of attention, we attempt to redesign familiar structures. In designing structures which balance arousal and repose we are at play. And because this occurs under always variable conditions, the structures we design are unavoidably variable, always moving between rigidity and amorphousness, heaviness and lightness.

Arrested by an illness, serving a sentence, bound by seemingly objective boundaries, we do what we can: we redefine our past, play basketball in wheelchairs, fantasize in solitary. We keep experimenting with ways for enriching the present by including fragments of the outside world within our confinements. We test possibilities and engage in negotiations to enlarge the range of action, to make exceptions into rules. In *The Kiss of the Spider Woman* (1985) two prisoners gropingly redesign the structure of their relationship, move toward embracing one another, and slowly cease to be imprisoned by what it means to act like men. They break a stereotype and learn to improvise like jazz musicians who are alert to unintended effects and unexpected sequences, as described by Donald Schon:

> Listening to one another and to themselves, they feel where the music is going and adjust their playing accordingly. . . . As the musicians feel the direction of the music that is developing out of their interwoven contribu-

> tions, they make new sense of it and adjust their performance to the new sense they have made. They are reflecting-in-action on the music they are collectively making and on their individual contributions to it, thinking what they are doing and, in the process, evolving their way of doing it.[18]

Using familiar melodic and harmonic structures, the musicians experiment with new ones—if only to amend them once expressed. The structures of their play are as temporary as the unspecified variations offered by a performer who, though attentive to the score, nevertheless imposes her distinctive timbre and coloring. While she or he depends on a masterful composer and a demanding instrument to express herself, she exploits the composer's and instrument's limitations, their residue of flexibility, their failure to confine her and finalize her performance. Her work consists of flirting with the given frame, of not submitting to it. Thus every sound she makes affirms and denies its context. When her composed derangements make more of life appear, she may of course worry about possible excesses and begin to retreat, tighten the frame of her expressions, adhere to classical forms and conventional ideals. As stimuli threaten to become overpowering, she moves to exclude them. Thus hers is an ongoing experiment, a continuous effort to identify the optimum tension between openness and closure. She accepts Milan Kundera's postulate: "If there is too much uncontested meaning on earth (the reign of the angels), man collapses under the burden; if the world loses all its meaning (the reign of the demons), life is every bit as impossible."[19] Her ultimate loyalty, it turns out, is to nothing but the growth of relationships; her discipline consists of orchestrating her impulse to agitate her environment and her contrary impulse to submit to it.

Weaving back and forth between grasping and letting go, she is the ungrounded child, the artist who allows herself to be astonished by the effects of her performances and uses them, as Anton Ehrenzweig has noted, to keep moving:

> The wood carver is delighted and not upset when the wood grain inside his block gradually reveals itself and by its obstinate twists compels

[18] Donald Schon, *The Reflective Practitioner* (New York: Basic Books, 1983), p. 55.

[19] Milan Kundera, *The Book of Laughter and Forgetting* (New York: Knopf, 1981), pp. 61, 11.

> him to modify his tentative ideas. . . . A new idea will inevitably be modified through its impact on the resisting medium. . . . The artist feels this need for expanding his point of departure and will welcome the independent life of his medium. Something like a true conversation takes place between the artist and his own work. The medium, by frustrating the artist's purely conscious intentions, allows him to contact more submerged parts of his own personality and draw them up for conscious contemplation. . . .
>
> The painter has hardly time to catch up with the floods of colour and to channel them into definite directions. Every touch of the brush that serves to dam the spreading may start a new flow somewhere else. The painter always remains one step behind his effort to keep up some measure of control, quite apart from the fact that he cannot entirely anticipate the change in colour by drying. . . . The skilled water-colourist watches the running of the colours with paper. . . . The accident is immediately incorporated into the artist's planning and to this extent becomes indistinguishable from his more intentional design.[20]

What had not been intended—what flows by itself—becomes part of the artist's design. Those uncanny forces we ordinarily keep off limits enrich his project, enhance his consciousness.

Yet there is no straightforward telling how much that is alien should be embraced by one's structures—one's very career. As we strive for increased comprehensiveness we can only ask ourselves how much we can bear at the moment. To how many antinomies of existence can we attend without flinching, without breaking? That this is no abstract, theoretical question is shown in Bertolt Brecht's *Galileo* when a monk reflects on a context which, for him, settles where the line should be drawn. His loyalties are divided between the aspirations of Galileo, whose assistant he is, and the concerns of the church, which does not wish to see the earth as it may be seen through Galileo's new telescope. The assistant reminds Galileo of the effect of his invention: the knowledge that the sun does not spin around the earth will surely frighten the peasantry, including the monk's own parents:

---

20 Anton Ehrenzweig, *The Hidden Order of Art: A Study in the Psychology of Artistic Imagination:* (Berkeley and Los Angeles: University of California Press, 1967), pp. 56–57.

> They scrape a living, and underlying their poverty there is a sort of order. There are routines. The routine of scrubbing the floors, the routine of the seasons in the olive orchard, the routine of paying taxes. . . . They draw the strength they need to sweat with their loaded baskets up the stony paths, to bear children, even to eat, from the sight of the trees greening each year anew, from the reproachful face of the soil, which is never satisfied, and from the little church and Bible texts they hear there on Sunday. They have been told that God relies upon them and that the pageant of the world has been written around them and that they may be tested in the important or unimportant parts handed out to them. How could they take it, were I to tell them that they are on a lump of stone ceaselessly spinning in empty space, circling around a second-rate star? What, then, would be the use of their patience, their acceptance of misery? What comfort, then, the Holy Scriptures, which have mercifully explained their crucifixion? The Holy Scriptures would then be proved full of mistakes. No, I see them begin to look frightened. I see them slowly put their spoons down on the table. They would feel cheated.[21]

Aware of a social context ignored by Galileo, the monk asks, "How could they take it?" It is one's view of the context, of course, that determines how far one should go, as Galileo himself realized when after being shown the instruments of torture he took account of his own limits, recanted, and thereby confirmed the structure of life offered by the church. He drew the line at what was, for him, the point of maximum manageable inclusiveness.

The same considerations determined the limits Bertolucci and his fellow film makers imposed on what became *Last Tango in Paris* (1973). They provided Marlon Brando with a stage on which to pull himself together and reconstruct his broken life. In a barely furnished Paris apartment Brando, never quite stripping, enlisted Maria Schneider to mark out a path toward wholeness in a space so open and empty that it would compel him to rely on his own resources for redemption, for moving beyond his mid-life crisis: "You don't have a name. Neither do I. No names . . . we don't need names here. Don't you see? We're going to forget

[21] Bertolt Brecht, *Galileo* (New York: Grove Press, 1966), p. 83.

everything we know—every—all the people all that we do—wherever we live. We are going to forget that, everything."[22] With no past and no code prescribing good form or fair play, Brando had but neutral space to design his own forms, his own rites of passage. While the camera framed his performance Brando slowly began to articulate a new life, a new structure for his experience—until Bertolucci, still the director aware of the tolerance of the movie's audience, declined to keep Brando's play going. He left Brando simply exhausted and purged, unprepared to live buoyantly. For those implicated in *Last Tango in Paris,* for film makers as well as audiences, the trip *through* primitivism was aborted. Bertolucci would not take Brando through terror and pain into an enlarged state of being. He simply showed Brando as unable to cope with modern history, with his middle-age crisis. Not allowing Brando to renew himself, Bertolucci indicated how far—given his cast, his audience, and his critics—it would be safe to go. Could he have stripped Brando and made him more vulnerable—and nonetheless shown him sufficiently composed to *articulate* a new life? Would filmmakers (including investors, actors, audiences, and critics) have remained composed? Would we (all of us) have remained at play?

The question remains pressing even though no answer is available outside a process within which we continuously reassess how much inclusiveness we are willing to risk. There is no transhistorical, transcultural authority to tell us whether we have gone too far or not far enough. Our limits are knowable only in the very transactions in which our lives are constituted. They are made manifest when we face a bottomless abyss, when we confront a world which, as an English anthropologist in India found himself instructed, rests on a platform which rests on the back of an elephant which rests on the back of a turtle. When the anthropologist inquired what the turtle rested on, he was told, "Another turtle." And that one? "Ah, Sahib, it is elephants and turtles all the way down." In this account the reality which our concepts frame has no preordained boundaries. The last creature is but the one to which we cling, the one we ourselves decide had better be final. When we are convinced that we have reached the end, we can forgive ourselves: after all, who has the energy,

---

[22] See Bernardo Bertolucci's *Last Tango in Paris* (New York: Delacorte Press, 1973).

skill, and wit to keep moving through infinity? There is no home amidst mirrors that release all our projects in endless reflections. We tire, drop out of the community, and cease to play. Having circulated enough, we simply end—or, *calling* an end to things, express our loyalty to a way of dying that we have designed for ourselves.

WE EVADE DEATH—oblivion—when we interact with those of the world's powers which, once touched and expressed, combine their vitality with ours. The difficulty is that we get to know our resources for such maneuvering only when we draw on them, as we learn to walk by walking or, less precisely, as we reduce the distance between an abstract notion of what it means to act and being in action. Whereas we know capacities that we have put to use, our unused potential can be known only in the process of activating ourselves and others—as Winston Churchill did when he enlisted himself and his compatriots to survive England's darkest hour. Success in such politics demands the performer's detachment from the dregs of empiricism, from what he has come to know excessively well: the results of past action. To change these results—the prevailing patterns of behavior—he must distrust what he knows; that is, he must free himself from the epistemology of empiricism by treating all evidence as mere provocation. Accepting no fixed definition of reality, he is loyal only to an unsymbolized whole in which to live is to die, in which the process of dying is intrinsic to living. Ambivalent toward all divided segments of experience, toward all parts being played, the performer's commitment, in short, is to endless play itself.

Obviously, the heavier the parts one seeks to enact, the more difficult it is to honor this commitment. The actor's self-discipline must be the more severe the more deeply he moves toward embracing any specific role. He can allow himself to be carried away by his acts only insofar as he remains detached enough to take the larger view and comprehend his actions. "I don't believe actors who say they *become* the part," Ingrid Bergman once noted; "you are, to some extent carried away . . . but you are always there. . . . Creating a role is like making a point—it is separate from you."[23] To remain in action you can't allow yourself to become

[23] Ingrid Bergman, quoted by Lillian Ross, "The Player," *New Yorker,* October 28, 1961, p. 112.

either master or slave, good or evil, attractive or ugly. You may embody merely as much of a role as you can control. On the one hand, your role may be so undemanding, so light and trivial, that it requires little self-control. Some parts, like some love affairs, engage so few of one's interests that the threat of *falling* in love is slight and there's no need for remaining on guard. But on the other hand, as a role makes heavier demands on you and ceases to be a mere *part,* the risk of self-abandonment increases: the movement toward death accelerates. The more heavily the actor is tested, the greater the risk of his losing his balance, his very consciousness. He knows that in the end, worn out by the steadiness of the limelight, he will lose his mind and submit to some form of Being. Forever deciding how deeply to move into treacherous territory, he keeps practicing how to die.

The courage it takes to remain detached from the parts one plays, especially those said to have been scripted by God, may be seen in what was Pastor Dietrich Bonhoeffer's final act. Just before his execution for treason in 1944, his Nazi jailors offered to let him conduct a last religious service in his cell. Knowing that his cellmate, a Soviet officer, was an atheist, he rejected the offer, declaring he had no interest in a religious ceremony. Without *becoming* a nonbeliever, Bonhoeffer acted as one. He kept his distance from this world as well as the next one, from the claims of expediency as well as those of principle—while responding to both. In his agony, he followed the dictum of his own theological writings that to remain alive to the needs of others honors God more fully than any specific act that presumes to give full expression to one's faith. At the end, nothing in particular, no determinate pronouncement attributed to God, was ultimate. What mattered were the endless, living claims of the phenomena impinging on one's consciousness. What mattered was to keep enacted life from ending. And to maintain that end alone, Bonhoeffer became deceptive: coming to terms with his fellow prisoner, he played a role and complicated his journey. He made life more inclusive.[24]

The history we know denies that human beings can ordinarily manage to extend their lives without faith in some indubitable reality. Only certified saints and imposters of fiction testify to the possibility of

---

[24] On Bonhoeffer's restraint, see John Murray Cuddihy, *The Ordeal of Civility* (New York: Basic Books, 1974), pp. 237–38, and Peter L. Berger, "Camus, Bonhoeffer and the World Come of Age," *Christian Century,* April 15, 1959, p. 452.

action fortified by nothing but its own ineffable dynamism. No one else, we claim, can dispense with institutionalized forms. Christ's kiss of the church's Grand Inquisitor serves to confirm our need for some institutionalized ideal which provides *real* standards, which incarnates and reifies what Dostoyevsky summarized as "miracle, mystery, and authority" and which produces the quiet terror administered by immigration officers, admissions committees, licensing boards, and art juries—all death squads scrupulously attentive to the ends of action, to completed work.

The closer we move toward some nameless Other, the more difficult it becomes to save ourselves by not narrowing the ends of action, that is, by continuing to equivocate and remain in suspense. Up against the impersonal rationality which is engineering a society whose members accept the increasingly precise computation of their fate, threatened by a painlessly spreading leukemia which numbs as it metastasizes, we cease to mediate. We have no language, no form of politics, for coming to terms with waves so quiet and so gentle. Near the edge we at most take note of the techniques by which we are moved toward a state in which even the most ingenious responses to one's fate become irrelevant, in which all conventional acts of heroism, decency, and caution are superfluous because they cease to make a difference. Whatever one's actions, they are either suicidal or contributions to ungoverned force. Such movies of the late 1980s as *Platoon, Hamburger Hill,* and *Full Metal Jacket* show that *every* choice is wrong, *all* exits lead to the same end.

It dawns on us—not only on teen-age soldiers in Vietnam—that to act at all in such a world is to be engaged in an exercise of futility. Betrayed by our own ideals, knowing the uselessness of even the best of formalities, we lash out and seek to terminate whatever band of postmodernist players fiddles while the gods remain silent and the city is imperceptibly eroding. As we frantically struggle against an all-pervasive technology we attempt to strike through the masks and artifices of postmodernists and recover the rock-bottom truth.

Postmodernists who succeed in holding such frenzy at bay engage in the kind of praxis which is so close to the process of reality that it is barely distinguishable from it. During the 1970s the bleached out, deadpan muteness of Andy Warhol showed how it might be done: "If you want to know all about Andy Warhol," he remarked, "just look at the surface of my paintings and films and me—and there I am. There's nothing behind it." His persona absorbed reality in appearance as it cruised through a world in which, as his Pop art insisted, nothing mattered and anybody could do anything, in which, as his most memorable remark had it, everyone could be famous for fifteen minutes. Alive to the irreversibility of the prevailing course, such performers follow the resourcefull pilot who in Stanley Kubrick's *Dr. Strangelove* obeys instructions to the letter, keeps his plane on course, and like the rest of his crew takes pains to deliver the bomb. Not mechanized, he decides not to let the world end of its own accord but to *make* it end. Not changing the outcome, he but amplifies it.

Following Kubrick's pilot, following Kubrick himself, we resist the thrust of modernity by telling a story, by producing narratives that elaborately depict the drift of events as the sublime unfolding of the inevitable. For the postmodernist near the end it turns out that the one voice left for engaging an unleashed technology is that of irony.

6 OUTDISTANCING REALITY

WHEN there's no way out, the voice of irony, shading into despair, remains one's last recourse for remaining alert and composed. What is left other than irony when, as we say, one's hands are tied, when one is convinced there is no escape from a cancerous growth or an armaments race? Near panic, you can only report "that's how it is"—and, while awaiting the end, elaborate on the "how" and the "it." "So it goes," Kurt Vonnegut repeats after relating each of the disasters he depicts in *Slaughterhouse Five*. Lucjan Dobroszyck's *Chronicle of the Lodz Ghetto* dispenses with judging the behavior of either victims or killers. There's no point in complaining, explaining, contradicting, blaming, or fretting. There's nothing to reverse: things can't be otherwise. In the face of unequivocal experience, one's language becomes uninflected, matter-of-fact, dry. What is absent in one's accounts are expressions of indignation. One's performances leave no room for the possibility that alternatives are available.

However unobtrusively, modernists had been indignant opponents of the dominant culture of the West. Implicitly committed to ideals of social justice and personal virtue, they were at odds with modernity.

Whether they believed their ideals to be expressed by lost myths, languages, and rituals, by nature or history, or by God or his prophets, modernists assumed the presence of a basis for their critique of the way history had been moving since the Enlightenment. Yet as they assailed the ugliness, banality, mendacity, corruption, incoherence, and perversion of the present day, they scarcely felt a need to give voice to this basis. For their public as well, right and wrong remain self-evident: Bacon's paintings depict obvious distortions of the human figure, Picasso's "Guernica" exposes a manifestly horrendous state, Hopper's view of urban loneliness, it goes without saying, is a plea for an absent community, Segal's super-realist sculptures of course condemn the context in which they appear, Orwell's *Nineteen Eighty-Four* dramatizes the opposite of what everyone—everyone—knows to be the just society.

Grounded and assured, modernists inhabited or at least identified with bohemian communities outside the gates of the modernizing state. Patronized in the salons of the bourgeoisie, tolerated by the politics of liberalism, and certain about the qualities of the center which was holding no longer, they knew themselves to be defending a transhistorical ideal of Normalcy and Humanism without having to insist on it. They were fortified by an ideal that justified their rebellion and held out hope for a New Jerusalem (in which Futurists included the machine). Thus modernists put modernity at risk by depicting its seemingly self-evident wastelands and horrors, perversions and abnormalities. In the Promethean spirit of Romanticism, they engaged in exploration and experimentation, assailed the life-destructive demands of industry and its markets, reached for the new in feeling and thought—and at the same time remained confident that the new (which as often as not idealized ancient structures now in ruins) could be established beyond the intolerable present. To them, the forces of history seemed pliable enough to yield to the politics of modernism: it was possible to escape the prisons of modernity. Although their designs represented the world's disruptions they nudged us toward an open window. Unlike the structures of postmodernism they held out the promise of order outside.

In America, postmodernist works began to surface when it became apparent that the sublime technology of Auschwitz and Hiroshima terminated saints and sinners at random, that the killing fields of Vietnam and

Cambodia revealed the futility of individual heroism and cost-benefit analyses, that bureaucratic managerialism was absorbing politics. A postmodernist sensibility took hold when writers, artists, and performers began to realize that the modernists' battle with a technique-centered, all-normalizing state was in the process of ending, when it became evident that works of art, far from being the adversaries of an instrumentalist, market-oriented society, were beoming its auxiliaries. The countercultural experiments of modernism, it became clear, were becoming cultural. John F. Kennedy's White House was co-opting the difficult "high art" of Frost and Stravinsky while the initially disturbing images of Magritte's paintings became comforting background for TV commercials. Opposition appeared pointless.

Unlike American modernists such as Saul Bellow, Cynthia Ozick, and John Updike, the postmodernist refers to no place outside the culture. There are no subsurface meanings which cushion her work. Appearances are all-permeating. Yet she maintains her independence by keeping her distance from the inescapable cultural momentum. To persist as self-reflective individual within an all-embracing state, she accepts modernity, generously paying tribute to its downbeat excitements, including (most ironically of all) the countercultural relics of modernism. At best, she could be an embrace untainted by resentment.

FRIEDRICH NIETZSCHE AND Henry Adams were but the first to disclose how to pay tribute to modernity while acknowledging its dreadful inhibitions.[1] For them, the sole option—Nietzsche and Adams exercised it vigorously—was to *make* the most of whatever forces impinged on them, forces which, in the form of technology, they both saw as inexorably increasing. The complexity of their lives and their work, the richness of their multigenred performances prefigured the postmodernist's combination of unalterable pessimism and the resolve to express it fully. They were at once resigned and passionate, lucid connoisseurs of the abyss and

[1] The parallel of Nietzsche and Adams, suggested by Leo Strauss (who also added Veblen), has moved me to treat Adams as elaborate role player: "The Limits of Social Science: Henry Adams' Quest for Order," *American Political Science Review* 50 (December 1956): 1974–92.

energetic publicists of its dimensions. Detached and yet purposeful, they acknowledged the inconsequence of their determination, the impotence of irony.

The postmodernist's ironic posturing is more than a flat, purposeless telling about the way things are. As the narrator attends to his subject, his endeavor is fueled by that surplus of energy for which the reality he confronts barely leaves room. In Georg Konrad's *The Case Worker* (1978) he becomes the social worker whose overwhelming case load in the lower depths of Budapest inspires verbal reveries of the futility of his labors. Sisyphus in Camus's account, Paul Newman in *Cool Hand Luke*, and Jack Nicholson in *One Flew over the Cuckoo's Nest* all resign themselves to their situations—and yet enact their sentences in a spirit of buoyant purposefulness which contradicts their victimization. None of them *had* to serve time so elaborately. None was *forced* to treat his surroundings with indiscriminate appreciation of its sheer presence. Adding to their troubles by doing deliberately what they could not escape doing, they seized space for action scarcely visible to those more thoroughly absorbed by their fate.

Whatever the setting of ironic performances, their authors show themselves to be in control. They slyly intimate, as Orson Welles and George Scott have done in TV commercials, that although one may be suffocating within a commercial culture, it remains possible to display an excess of spirit which, not being demanded, is freely chosen. Within an economy that provides him with only meager roles, an aging Laurence Olivier flaunts his surplus energy and talent; accepting the fixed expectations of the entertainment system, he does things better than his script demands. Alec Guinness as the British colonel compelled to build the bridge on the river Kwai proceeds with exaggerated efficiency. These actors out of breath still manage to proclaim their independence. Seeing them perform, we realize they *comprehend* what is scarcely comprehensible. If they have intimate knowledge of alien forces, this is because they have embraced them. And yet while collaborating with their enemies they feel as spotless as Melville claimed he did after writing *Moby-Dick*. Irritating those who hold out hope for reform, they are serene in the midst of disaster. They have decided to stop worrying, to go along with society's destructive instruments, to add their own weight to that of the bomb, and, straddling it like the Texan pilot in *Dr. Strangelove, or How to Stop Worrying and Love the Bomb,* to ride it down cheering. Believing annihilation is irrevocably ahead in any case, they escape being victims of the prevailing powers by taking charge of themselves, of what life remains. Refusing to make judgments, they use what energy they have left, play as fully as they can, and allow an absent God to judge the consequences.

At the same time their amoral, ironic tone and their paradox-saturated practices constitute, in Malraux's durable metaphor, museums without walls. Constructing dwelling places to shelter whatever they remove from its prior context, they create the visible works of postmodernism—hospitable collages and assemblages, each so barely framed that their contents blend into their environment, each a refuge for found objects, each redeeming the discards and shadows of modernity. In the end, they strain to present content-free matrixes like Sol Le Witt's *Modular Cube Series (19690176),* Mondrian's grids, Reinhardt's frameworks, or Albers's structures.

The designers of such permeable, open-ended structures careen through contradictory genres, relish the absence of secure points of view, and deprive every subject of its ontological status. Their most radical contemporary guide, Jacques Derrida, projects a convoluted imagery which mocks the ground he stands on. Knowing himself to be a prisoner of the forms of language, he feverishly seeks to outperform them in barely controlled joy rides—rides which few will pay to join. Likewise, Barth, Elkin, Boyle, Barthelme, Gaddis, Calvino, Borges, Coover, Nabokov, Warhol, Gass, Eco, Burroughs, Carver, Pynchon—it has become easy to drop their names—appeal to no alternative utopia, to nothing of substance.[2] Heroically unheroic, they put their very identity at risk. Their careers tolerate no definitive obituary. Presupposing no golden age in the past or future, they treat everything, including themselves, as present—or, rather, as capable of being *made* present by changes in style, genre, form, context, perspective, and interpretation, by whatever it takes, not to change the institutions of modernity, an impossible task, but to outperform them.

---

[2] For a discriminating discussion of writers as postmodernists, see Charles Russell, *Poets, Prophets, and Revolutionaries* (New York: Oxford University Press, 1987), chap. 8.

To delineate the nuances and ramifications of the forces which depress them, they become the most voracious of appropriators. They put reality in quotes, as Philip Taafee does in his painstaking reproductions of the British artist Bridget Riley. Surrendering everything of substance to the process of consumption, they put an end to Art. They offer nothing authentically original. Thus in one of her projects Sherrie Levine has simply rephotographed the art-book reproductions of Edward Weston's familiar photographs, made prints of them, and exhibited her work. Ignoring the conventions of private property, she has similarly recycled the canonized legacy of Walker Evans's famous Farm Security Administration photographs. In the 1980s she offered a series of exhibits that questioned the originality of authorship—and by inference the very possibility of being original. By dismissing all pretense of originality and engaging in a process that crushed private property as effectively as the modernizing process of corporate power, she enacted what is taking place in the world at large. And anticipating the future, she may, like Laurie Anderson, create publicity handouts as willfully inclusive as the following flyer:

> HOME OF THE BRAVE
> USA 1986
> Written, directed, and conceived by Laurie Anderson
> With Laurie Anderson, William Burroughs, Adrian Belew,
> and others
> Color 90 min.
>
> "*My work is a combination of film, music, electronics, storytelling, dancing, social commentary, impersonation, animation, and anything else I come up with. What I do has been described as 'high-tech opera,' 'lively art,' 'electronic stand-up comedy,' 'avant rock,' and that clumsy label 'performance art,' which has always sounded to me like a bad translation from German. I have this vision of myself as part of a long tradition of American humor—you know, Bugs Bunny, Daffy Duck, Road Runner. . . .*"— LAURIE ANDERSON.

Laurie Anderson, who has brought intermedia performance art to its largest mass audience, has been called precocious by some and hailed as an electronic explorer creatively expanding the boundaries of contemporary media. Her enormously popular videos, such as SHARKEY'S MACHINE, blend music, dance, poetry, and comedy with exhilarating animation reminiscent of Max Fleischer. Her first feature film, HOME OF THE BRAVE, adds painting, sculpture, computer graphics, Dada, kabuki, and noted musicians to the heady mixture. With the help of cinematographer John Lindley, an electronic wizard, editor Lisa Day, and fashion designer Susan Hilferty, who supplies wonderfully idiosyncratic costumes, Anderson carries several media at once into a brand-new sphere, perhaps into a brand-new century.

A year and a half in the making, HOME OF THE BRAVE, was filmed in Union City, New Jersey, at the Park Theater, an auditorium built to present passion plays. It captures Anderson and her special guests in a performance of their critically acclaimed 1984 MISTER HEARTBREAK stage show, whose songs were influenced by such diverse figures as Thomas Pynchon, William Shakespeare, and William Burroughs. Anderson cites Rainer Fassbinder, Jean-Luc Godard, and Alan Rudolph among her cinematic influences.

HOME OF THE BRAVE is one of the first feature-length films to be recorded and mixed digitally (a 24-track studio was built on the film site) and marks the first time in history that a synchronous feature-length movie has been released in pure digital sound.

Says *Vogue* magazine, *"Anderson . . . has created a kind of gorgeous technological paradise. If* HOME OF THE BRAVE *sounds too artsy for words, it's not. The most compelling aspect of the films is how much fun everyone seems to be having.*

"If STOP MAKING SENSE *was the* BMW *of the hip-hop litmus tests,* HOME OF THE BRAVE *is the Rolls Royce."—New York Daily News*

"Impeccable . . . dreamlike visual poetry." *Newsday*

A VERITABLE CATCH-ALL, this ad for Laurie Anderson's "technological paradise" touches all postmodernist bases.[3] It shows her straining to

[3] Like Anderson's, the projects of the Talking Heads and David Byrne (especially *True Stories* [1986]), David Lynch, Beth Henley, and Robert Wilson are cases in point. Their

be comprehensive—to accredit all her predecessors, to remember it all, to recall, recycle, and commemorate. Defying the dictates of good taste and those who define it, she's indifferent to the presumed quality of what she brings into relationships. An unabashed plagiarist, endlessly lip-syncing, she's a wholly medium-oriented mediator responsible only for relating what she's encountered. Undermining the conventions of ownership and authorship, she obscures the distinction between what she herself has made up and what she's absorbed from her surroundings. As inventive as the modern corporation, she quotes out of context and inserts the quotes in her production. Lowering the barrier between inside and outside, she admits society's outcasts without sanitizing them. Of course we assure ourselves that *Home of the Brave* is "only a movie," and we add that surely there's a real world outside where one's overparked car is really being ticketed. Yet in her unreal world—in mine as well—the meaning of events is created by the frame in which they are placed—a frame in which the ticketing of cars can be cherished as a spectacular exhibit of rectitude, fastidiousness, and precision, in which everything is celebrated because it has appeared.

Jon Kessler's kinetic sculpture has been appreciated by Kim Levin on the same grounds:

> He takes failed elements of the old Art and Technology stuff from the late '60s and makes them work. . . . Four of the pieces in his current show are elaborately programmed on digital computers . . . but they still got all the improvised mechanical gizmos, lightbulbs, and plastic toys exposed at the sides so you can see, voyeuristically, what makes them tick. Because the pieces posess the right combination of skills and gaucheries, the technology doesn't overwhelm the art. . . . Nourished by artificialities and simulations, he has an appetite for the trite and the debased. Encompassing the trivialized present and the popularized past, reminding us constantly of art (Kim MacConnel lurks in his '50s fabric pattern, Charles Simonds in the miniaturized bit of landscape, Chris Burden in the toys), his atrophied

---

multimedia performances which manipulate and hype advertised images provide no ground for including or excluding anything. In their postmodern universe nothing is at stake, nothing contradicts anything else.

images brim with hysteria as well as kitch historicism. . . . His work is a window onto unreality, a screen on which to project.[4]

To idealize the process in which Anderson produced her film and Kessler his sculpture is to see it supported by their installations—unbounded installations that serve to facilitate an ongoing activity of re-presenting re-pairing, re-deeming, re-newing, re-defining, re-butting, re-affirming, re-leasing, re-adjusting, re-capitulating, re-vitalizing, re-habilitating, re-minding, re-producing, re-questing, re-searching, re-solving, re-membering, re-fining, re-collecting, re-imbursing, re-funding, re-citing, re-forming, re-juvenating, re-installing, re-moving, re-constructing, re-novating, re-playing, re-cycling, re-grouping, re-dressing, re-trieving. Leaving nothing intact, this endless process takes place on revolving platforms at the vertiginous heights not of Plato's final insights but of his endless dialogues, not of Einstein's scientific conclusions but of his inconclusive mental experiments—all playful performances which keep refilling the void.

THE DETERMINATION TO engage in an ever-shifting, open-ended politics to keep structures from becoming definitive becomes especially manifest in the products of postmodernist architecture. The architecture of modernism had been an uncompromising one of high principle. Following the chaos of the First World War, its structures (especially those which never got off the drawing board) proclaimed that form follows function, that ornament must be sacrificed to the delocalized, denationalized purity of what came to be called an International Style.[5] In the postmodernist architecture which emerged after the Second World War, form no less follows function—but function is perceived not as international or univer-

---

[4] Kim Levin, "High-Tech Chow Mein," *Village Voice,* November 5, 1985, p. 98. Frank Stella's output emerges as postmodernist in Adam Gopnik's review of a retrospective exhibit of his relief paintings. Gopnik characterizes Stella's overloaded three-dimensional, high-tech constructions as appropriating and ornamenting the world as is, including all its "kitch detritus." He speaks of their "greedy vitality, their materialism, their love of cheap sensation (not to mention their essentially unheroic ambitions, even a certain complacency). . . . " ("Stella in Relief," *New Yorker,* January 4, 1986, pp. 70–73.)

[5] On the totalizing, purifying thrust of modernism, see Frank Lentricchia, *Ariel and the Police: Michel Foucault, William James, Wallace Stevens* (Madison: University of Wisconsin Press, 1987).

sal but as local, that is, as diverse, historical, and contradictory, as immanent in close-at-hand desires, fads, and preoccupations. Not operating under the banner of a singular ideology, it defies reduction to purity, logic, coherence. Appealing to no truth outside the imperium of modernity, it cheerfully pays tribute to the cost accountant's demand for computer-designed, optimum-efficiency structures, doing so with that excess of exuberance which signals a desperate effort to remain in control. It works, as Charles Moore said of his buildings, only "to freshen one's perception of the familiar." If it declines to change the familiar world and its markets, it intensifies awareness of them. Thus Helmut Jahn's 1986 United Airlines terminal at Chicago's O'Hare airport—an inordinately efficient, gleaming and glistening Victorian railway station—is at once an enthusiastic affirmation of a people-regimenting, people-moving technology and a design which draws travelers into a travel-is-painless fantasy. For Jahn a self-serving "service" economy is as much an irrevocable fact as the glitzy commercial strip of Las Vegas is for Robert Venturi. Resigned to this fact, he makes it express more than it demands. Where modernists like Le Corbusier strip their structures of "dysfunctional" ornamentation, postmodernists ironically embellish and heighten the meretriciousness of a culture whose privileged functionaries are absorbed by facades that constitute readymade life styles.

The postmodernist's design becomes what Charles Jencks has defined as "double coded." In 1977, Jencks perceived postmodernist architecture as relating the modern and the traditional, the professional and the popular.[6] In a later study he singled out James Sterling's addition to the Staatsgalerie, a museum in Stuttgart, as exemplifying double coding:

> The u-shaped palazzo form of the old gallery is echoed and placed on a high plinth or acropolis above the traffic. But his classical base holds a very real and necessary parking garage, one that is ironically indicated by stones which have "fallen," like ruins, to the ground. The resultant holes in the "Acropolis" show the real construction, which is steel frame holding stone cladding, not the thick marble blocks of the real Acropolis, and they allow the air ventilation required by law. One can sit on these false ruins and ponder the truth of our lost innocence: that we live in an age which can

[6] Charles Jencks, *The Language of Post-Modern Architecture* (New York: Rizzoli, 1977). See also Heinrich Klotz, *Postmodern Visions* (New York: Abbeville Press, 1985).

> build with beautiful, expressive masonry as long as we make it skin deep and hang it on a steel skeleton.

Sterling's is a hybrid grammar wholly at odds with the modernist's insistence on "truth to materials," "logical consistency," and "simplicity."[7] Like other postmodernists, Sterling has spun a web which catches contradictory parts and allows them to appear in all their distinctiveness. Having recycled art forms of the past, he himself has created nothing other than the relation between the parts he assembled—his array of clichés, of already known styles, fashions, fixtures. Whatever he has constructed, it announces no particular goal as one he intended to reach. He is all but the nameless, faceless bureaucrat, that vacant presence which Andy Warhol made of himself. Wherever intentionality may be located, his work fails to present it. Conventional criticism is disarmed: no pealing back of the surface of the text can disclose its central point. The text, as Roland Barthes has said, does not release the author's message. It is but a "multi-dimensional space in which are married and contested several writings, none of which is original: the text is a fabric of quotations, resulting from a thousand sources of culture."[8]

If the projects of postmodernism dramatize the endless seriality, intertextuality, and pastiche associated with the structures of modernity, they also lead to the realization that no one in particular can be identified as responsible for their effects. Their author-creator-originator is absent in the outpouring of mixed media and diverse genres. He is as unlocatable and anonymous as the decision makers of a fully developed technological society, as the unpronouncable God of negative theology and freewheeling feminism.[9] The verbal and palpable artifacts of culture—its very deities—are but factitious constructions which may appear or disappear, depending always on the limits of human resourcefulness for designing a world which holds them captive.

---

[7] Charles Jencks, "Post-Modern and Late-Modern: The Essential Definitions," unpublished paper, 1986.

[8] Roland Barthes, *The Rustle of Language* (New York: Hill and Wang, 1986), pp. 52–53.

[9] Some feminists join postmodernism in precisely this de-authorization of Authority. See Jacqueline Rose, "Sexuality in the Field of Vision," in Kate Linker, ed., *Difference: On Representation and Sexuality* (New York: New Museum of Contemporary Art, 1984).

THE POSTMODERNIST AGENT is of course not unaware of his limits. He knows that his energy must flag, that he can't be invariably ahead of reality. The magnitude of his problem is manifest: contemporary reality—as the evening news makes clear—is scarcely distinguishable from fiction. At world fairs, the exhibited technology puts the artist to shame. To be sure, there may be modest agitations. In 1986 dayglow bumperstickers proclaimed that EXPO '86 SUCKS and posters showed a mushroom cloud emerging above Vancouver's exposition compound. Yet the brilliance of the colors did little more than echo the prevailing hype. More invasively, Vancouver's Expo '86 was crossed by a four-block-long undulating strip called Highway 86—a dense array of buses, cars, boats, airplanes, and jogging shoes, some two hundred uniformly grey objects all facing the same direction, a plane emerging from water at one end and a car heading up a ramp into the sky at the other. But however inspired such efforts to outdistance a self-generating technology, at best they amount to witty commentaries. In a familiar *Atlantic Monthly* essay Philip Roth took note of the artist's predicament: "The American writer in the middle of the twentieth century has his hands full in trying to understand, and then describe, and then make *creditable* much of the American reality. It stupefies, it sickens, it infuriates, and finally it is even a kind of embarrassment to one's meager imagination. The actuality is continually outdoing our talents."

As Jean Baudrillard, a French poststructuralist, has argued, the signs and symbols of the present have ceased to signify and symbolize. When their meanings are utterly destabilized, they are as readily attached to instruments of destruction as to those of salvation. They no longer refer to anything beyond them—only to other signifiers and symbols. At that point the postmodernist is at the end, for modernity has become totalitarian and the artist can no longer frame reality.[10] He can't outplay an all-comprehensive cataclysm, use one or another yardstick, and dispas-

---

[10] The triumph of technicism is expressed at its most sublime in Heinrich Himmler's speech to a group of officers who commanded killing squads during World War II at Germany's eastern front. He exhorted them to suppress all sentiment and devote themselves to their task of exterminating Jews and partisans however much the task might pain them. (Nuremberg Document PS-1918, in *Nazi Conspiracy and Aggression* [Washington, D.C.: 1946–1948], vol. 4, pp. 558–78.)

sionately take the measure of the abyss emblemized as "Auschwitz." To account for "Auschwitz" is to give it a place within a larger, more comprehensive accounting system—which is to disavow its totality.

However totally history ended in the bottomless abysses of the twentieth century, we nonetheless persist in efforts to bring such Otherness to measure. We call it to account, responding to Karl Marx's exhortation to make "petrified social conditions . . . dance by singing their own melody to them."[11] We make a can of soup the centerpiece of a painting; we make the swishing of a windshield wiper the beat of a melody. We persist in remaining disengaged from the dominant culture whether as modernists implying alternatives to it or as postmodernists explicating its implicit dimensions. Space for ironic maneuver remains. Jeremy Bentham's utilitarian calculations have not been enacted; the bureaucratic organization Max Weber blueprinted have yet to be realized; George Orwell's 1984 has not arrived. As yet, people don't make their way through supermarkets as mechanically as George Segal's life-sized "Woman with Shopping Cart." Nor is any present technological empire as flawlessly self-regulating as Jean Baudrillard's constructions. In short, for both modernists and postmodernists, there is time and space for imposing an aesthetic perspective on the present, for contradicting and refining the facts of life and death, for following Greek dramatists who were detached enough to give expression to the nobility of their enemies.[12]

What distinguishes postmodernist displays of the unrealized realities of the present is the thoroughness of their aestheticizing practices, their readiness to make a preoccupation with style become their sole occupation. Determined to salvage the most repressive of forces, they can abide no form of reductionism, no pushing foreground into background. They will neither reduce a national park to a paradise for the virtuous (as

---

[11] Karl Marx, "The Critique of Hegel's Philosophy of Right," in *Early Writings* (London: C. A. Watts, 1963), p. 47.

[12] An aesthetic view is provided by Bruegel's treatment of "The Massacre of the Innocent," a happening whose horror is absent in the painting itself. It is suspended, as Eliot Deutsch has noted, "by our having to adopt the viewpoint of nature—a viewpoint which is indifferent to human events" and which rejects "the medieval 'dual realism' of a painter like Raphael." (Eliot Deutsch, *Studies in Comparative Aesthetics* [Honolulu: University Press of Hawaii, 1975], p. 43.)

in Ansel Adams's photograph of Yosemite Valley) nor reduce a suburb to a wasteland for the damned (as in Steven Shore's photographs of suburban vistas). And because there is always more to it, one's performances merit applause to the extent that they provide access to the unknown, to the reduced dimensions of experience.

Suspending moral judgment, the postmodernist proceeds the way David Lynch directed *Blue Velvet* (1986), a film more memorable for its style than its subject—merely another story of a high school graduate coming of age. Taking in the happy surface of a small American town, the camera intensifies the artifacts of suburbia from tulips to furniture, accentuating their every detail. The ordinary becomes extraordinary; familiar reality emerges as super-real. And beneath the town's eerie ordinariness the hero is led to encounter an inferno of sex and violence. As the character (and the audience) moves into and out of this supercharged world, Lynch brings the town's two sides into relationship. Free from moral constraints, he indiscriminately magnifies both, making everything equal on the screen. Only at the end does he make a comment, as if realizing that after leaving the theater his audience will fail to understand that the Happy Ending may as easily have been the reverse: a plump robin which lands on the kitchen windowsill slowly chews on an insect wriggling in its beak, and someone says without referring to anything in particular, "It's over now."

Having reached the end, Lynch calmly holds his all-intensifying mirror up to reality. Privileging neither bird nor insect, Lynch is the unruffled, indifferent performer who insinuates that fate is unalterably fate, that no one is in charge of morality. Absorbed by reality, he risks giving impetus to his own disappearance.

LYNCH MOVES WITH the self-assured nonchalance of the professional photographer at the scene of a disaster. At the edge of the human community, he sees what had remained invisible to others. His cool posture is that which Bertolt Brecht, reflecting on "Poor B. B.," attributes to himself:

> I gather some fellows around me towards evening:
> We address each other as "gentlemen."
> They put their feet on my table
> And say: things will improve. And I don't ask when.

For B. B.'s cronies—self-styled gentlemen who put their feet on his table—it is the end of the day, and all is deflated, all but the cadences of Brecht's language.

Within the discourse of irony, a divine impartiality relates contradictory ideals. Irony unites a bewildering welter of events while it dispenses with judgment—and the action judgment calls for. Not presuming to prescribe, merely illuminating with deadpan exactitude, it is but the playground of all-knowing survivors. They see what we ordinarily see—only more fully. Their experience has made them less squeamish in tracing the course of events, enabling them to see that everything implies its opposite. Unwilling to discriminate, denounced as relativists, their narratives allow human traumas to become comic—black instances of humanity's foibles.[13] They equalize all positions, as Robert Frost has done:

> I wouldn't give a cent to see the world, the United States or even New York much better. I want them left just as they are for me to make poetical on paper. I don't ask anything done to them that I don't do myself. I'm a mere selfish artist for the time. I have no quarrel with the material. The grief will be simply if I can't transmute it into poems. I don't want the world made safer for poetry or easier. To hell with it. That is its own outlook. Let it stew in its position while *I do it in art.* My whole anxiety is for myself as a performer.[14]

To do it in art, the performer is obliged to remain alert and lucid. His is a discipline that demands identifying with the very structures that threaten his effort to depict them. Tocqueville writing on equality, Kafka on organizational labyrinths, Veblen on the leisure class, Riesman on the

---

[13] "Try for a moment," Henri Bergson advises, "to become interested in everything that is being said and done; act, in imagination with those who act, and feel with those who feel; in a word give your sympathy its widest expansion; as though at the touch of a fairy wand you will see the flimsiest of objects assume importance, and a golden hue spread over everything. Now step aside, look upon life in a disinterested speculation: many a drama will turn into comedy. To produce the whole of its effect, then, the comic demands something like a momentary anesthesia of the heart." (Henri Bergson, *Laughter* [New York: Macmillan, 1921], pp. 4–5.)

[14] Robert Frost, quoted in Richard Poirier, *The Performing Self* (New York: Oxford University Press, 1970), p. 92 (my emphasis).

lonely crowd—all of them comprehend a reality deeper than the manifest one. Turning the process of modernity into deliberate constructions, they are mindful of forces others do not mind, forces which, when not poeticized, remain uncomprehended Otherness, brute power. These models of composure dare to make a record that is as free from outrage and rancor as films that appear to be documentaries. Thus Agnes Varda's evenhanded *Vagabond* (1985) indicts neither individuals nor institutions as it presents the story of Mona (Sandrine Bonnaire), an eighteen-year-old "without roof or law" (the French title of the film). Under the emptiest of skies, Mona drifts aimlessly through the wintry French countryside and ends dirty and exhausted in a ditch at the side of a road, a frozen body. The film's other characters, witnesses to the last weeks of her life, see her as a listless, sullen vagrant who did no more than react to whatever she encountered. Excluded by society, she is impenetrable, the camera's passive object. Nothing is shown to provide access either to her or her surroundings: it's *all* surfaces. Things are hopelessly what they are, and no one needs to be reminded, as Brecht's B. B. reminded his cronies, that things won't improve. Agnes Varda explains nothing. "I wanted to create a stimulating or bracing discomfort whereby the spectator shapes a portrait from fragments and realizes the film has no answer," she has said; "my primary subject was the phenomenon of those who die of the cold, outside and alone."

As director of *Shoah* (Hebrew for "extermination"), Claude Lanzmann no less created a context in which to come to terms with people "without roof or law"—children, women, and men deported, numbed, and exterminated. He no less generated "a stimulating or bracing discomfort whereby the spectator shapes a portrait from fragments and realizes the film has no answer." For some nine hours of screening Lanzmann provides visual views of various killing grounds and, with the help of an interpreter, elicits the testimony of survivors, technicians, railroad workers, bureaucrats, and bystanders who lived near the camps. Long pauses, tedious repetitions, and three intermissions give audiences a chance to construct meanings and explanations. The film projects, to use Hannah Arendt's precise noun, the banality of the Final Solution. The answers Lanzmann elicits from the survivors he interviews point not to the obsessive brutality of the Nazi regime but to its utterly coherent, rational, technologically implemented program. Just how preoccupied Lanzmann is by the technology for terminating human communities becomes clear when he relaxes and almost loses himself in what is left of the Jewish community of Corfu which is shown at prayer. But he quickly returns to his infinitely larger canvas—the ingenious fastidiousness of the organization of extermination. How, he wants to know, were Jews who had been living so far from the center of death so efficiently rounded up and dispatched? He is engaged in an inquest; he wants answers. Quietly but relentlessly, he asks witness after witness for the minutest of details ("what color were the vans?"). With Raul Hilberg, the holocaust historian-archivist whose words are as detached as Lanzmann's, he patiently reviews the schedules of the special trains that in the midst of war efficiently transported Jews to the death camps. Gently but unsparingly he brings everyone, including Jewish survivors who themselves became tools of the machinery of death, to the point of talking about their experience. His film implicates everyone but convicts no one—however much his audiences may resent his patience, his "mere" question-raising, his "failure" to take sides. He remains relaxed and amoral (he casually reveals the name and face of a Nazi functionary to whom he promises anonymity). After three years of work on the film, Lanzmann is a survivor for whom morally grounded transgressions have no meaning.

Shoah declines to be captivated by any specific occurrences between 1942 and 1945. Its particular elements—above all, the endless trains that bring their cargo to its destination—are but parts of an all-comprehensive process, one which, to be sure, does not engulf Lanzmann and his film crew, his audiences and his critics. Throughout his performance, he remains quietly in control. He never italicizes. During the time he has—the time he takes—he imposes order on chaos, on whatever future holocausts rest silently within the present, a present he keeps extending. After a Warsaw ghetto fighter recalls how well life went on for Poles outside, Lanzmann ignores the terror experienced by the Polish population under the German occupation and lets his camera scan the smooth surface of the Warsaw of the 1980s: the present contains past and future. There can be no de-Nazification, no laments, no atonement, no transcendence. It's all here now. He looks steadily at an incommensurable experience and locates it in an idyllic Polish landscape, a lyrical cliché that is surely the opposite of that indeterminate totality framed by his determination. What took place has no place. It is but a process, an echo without source, surely nothing that originated in the minds of Germans or the hearts of Poles. He seems reluctant to have the film end: it merely fatigues. He works as long as possible to deepen and extend the desolation he depicts; he persists in the midst of a universal cataclysm with his voice uncracked, his camera rolling.

Lanzmann's performance is also Akira Kurosawa's in *Ran* ("chaos"). Reenacting the tales of a sixteenth-century fratricidal war, Kurosawa shows himself coming to terms—cinematic terms, to be sure—with a life devoid of meaning. Following *King Lear,* he imposes the grammar of film to tell the story of an old man's quest for meaning within an uncomprehended, unframed war. War and recoil from it—that's all there is. To enable his audiences to *see* the clash of armies, Kurosawa silences their clashing armor and the screams of the wounded before he immerses the carnage in music. In the scene of a decapitation, blood drips as artfully from a screen in the background (we do not see the victim) as paint from a Jackson Pollack canvas. Kurosawa imposes a spectacular order on chaos, a chaos absorbed in his design, his performance. Opening with a scene of a boar being brought to its end by a hunting party, the film closes with a view of a young man who, sightless at the edge of a precipice, has lost his flute, his relation to the transcendent reality of Buddhism, his last tie to another human being, and the path back to law and order. Kurosawa ends as he begins, steadied only by his will to construct a reality in the midst of others who might have the discipline to join him.

DOCUMENTING AN EXECUTION, the photographer's camera remains as steady as he is: he and the camera are at one. Neither acknowledges anything that might disrupt their singular function. They shed no tears. Pure media, their operation is seamless. They neither weep nor laugh. Both are oblivious to those who resent their knowledge, their innocence, their equanimity.

Remembering his childhood, John Updike speaks of himself as an "experiencer"—is it God as ironist?—and recalls a specific moment of exhilaration. It was a moment during which he experienced

> deep, cosmic joy [in] the sensation of shelter, of being out of the rain. The experiencer is motionless holding his breath as it were, and the things

> experienced are morally detached from him: there is nothing he can do, or ought to do, about the flow, the tumult. He is irresponsible, safe, and witnessing. . . . There was nothing cruel about crouching in a shelter and letting phenomena slide by: it was ecstasy. The essential self is innocent, and when it tastes its own innocence knows that it lives forever. If we keep utterly still, we can suffer no wear or tear, and will never die.[15]

Godlike in our innocence, we stay motionless. Being everywhere, we need not move. As unmoved and as self-sufficient as Plato's ideal philosopher, we deny our mortality and accept ourselves as all-powerful in our boundless love of all being.

Touching infinity, irony negates itself and becomes the only voice that can still be heard.

---

[15] John Updike, "A Soft Spring Night in Shillington," *New Yorker,* December 24, 1984.

7 RECOILING FROM IRONY

THE pleasures and pains displayed by an actor are not his own. In fact, he himself seems bothered by nothing. Unlike him, however, you know pleasure and pain to be yours, and take action to alleviate what assuredly is pain, to enhance what assuredly is pleasure. When he makes light of his difficulties, you discern a streak of perversity in his makeup, as you do in the deflated language of the mountaineer:

> The most arduous and hair-raising climbs, dangers, tribulations, and personal injuries are discussed in dispassionate terms. Frightful peril becomes a "very committing" situation. Tiny holds on sheer walls thousands of feet up pose a "problem," an "awkward passage" is "interesting." The broken finger or leg or other injury is "quite bothersome."[1]

As I am jogging uphill and beginning the final stretch toward home, I use the same language. A neighbor standing on the side of the road stops working on his car, looks up, and grins at me. "How you doing?" he says.

---

[1] Richard G. Mitchell, Jr., *Mountain Experience* (Chicago: University of Chicago Press, 1983), p. 69.

Sub specie aeternitatis, everything's all right. Whatever my pain it doesn't hold my interest. I take a global view and say, "doing fine." I am home by the time I reflect on my equanimity. Could I honestly have thought that I'm fine and all is well?

Once home I'm certainly no actor ready to embrace God's perspective. Normally, I try to improve things and reject the actor's posture. I won't assume that it's pointless to straighten things out, that life is skidding out of control, that we are all irreversibly in motion. Surely there is time to work on better roads, to build less destructive vehicles, to train more skillful drivers, or at least to improve medical technology for those who crash.

Declining to be fatalistic and recognizing that the filigree of irony screens out the very rage which fuels reform, we want to *do* something about the oppressive reality to which irony submits. Our idealism intact, we resent the failure (as we call it) of the ironist to move outside his discourse and raise his voice in protest against the evils of the day. We resent Robert Venturi's cool way of filming the strip of casinos at Las Vegas—his asking his students of architecture to take it all in, to acknowledge it fully, to ignore its moral impact on others.

In aestheticizing the present the ironist deprives it of that larger moral context on which we continue to insist. After all, we regard the amorality of irony as pathological as long as the world continues to allow for change. We are irritated by performances as seamless as Michel Foucault's self-contained narratives. Little in the way we view our experiences allows us to believe that language leaves no room for indignation, that it generates itself. We are irritated by the narrator's controlled account of the way the rest of us are out of control, imprisoned by our habits.

What we react to is the elitism we attribute to the ironist—his tenacious way of calling attention to everyone else's defeat by reality.[2] Like a doctor monitoring a terminal case, he seems fascinated by alien power. Again and again, a touch of virulent pleasure marks his voyeristic reports: individuals are inexorably and exquisitely locked into Weber's "iron cage," Goffman's "total institutions," or Foucault's "panoptic ma-

[2] The elitism of Foucault's discourse is suggested in Peter Dews, "The Nouvelle Philosophy and Foucault," *Economy and Society* 8 (May 1979): 125–76.

chine." Individuals are depicted as submerged and twisting, as helplessly caught in some field of forces. Detached from their pathetic struggles, the ironist conducts himself with the self-assured nonchalance of the professional photographer at the scene of a disaster. At the fringe of the human community, he knows others to inhabit a world which he manages to see fully. *They* move in a darkness unaware of the pathos of their lives, the falseness of their hopes. Exulting in displaying the condition of others, he betrays his appetite for power even as he embraces the world from his poststructuralist viewpoint, a retreat located beyond all specific structures. Did he earn his equanimity?

HOWEVER AFFRONTED, WE are nonetheless attracted by the dexterity with which the ironist paints the darkness at the edge of our lives. Braced to hear him, we may find relief by laughter, as Thomas Mann recalls when at a small party Kafka was read aloud. We pay to attend his performance. Reading Nietzsche, we treat his work as hyperbole and detach ourselves from his notorious provocations: "What in us really wants truth? Suppose we want truth: *why not rather* untruth? and uncertainty? even ignorance?" He pushes further: "To suffer does one good, to see others suffer even more: this is a hard saying but an ancient, mighty, human, all-too-human principle. . . . Without cruelty there is no festival." And: "I call Christianity the one great curse, the one innermost corruption, the one great instinct of revenge, for which no means is poisonous, stealthy, subterranean, *small* enough—I call it the one immortal blemish of humanity."[3] There's something in what he says, we think, but not everything. Having heard him, we turn to less unnerving subjects.

Hearing Lenny Bruce's nightclub performance or seeing George Segal's trompe-l'oeil sculpture of a life-size art museum visitor who has collapsed at the top of the stairs of the National Gallery's new wing, we head home. We don't regard ourselves as mere victims—as members of the bourgeoisie who helplessly contribute to the demise of their class, as

---

[3] Friedrich Nietzsche, *Beyond Good and Evil,* in *The Portable Nietzsche,* trans. Walter Kaufmann (New York: Viking Press, 1954), p. 1; *On the Genealogy of Morals,* trans. Walter Kaufmann and J. R. Hollingdale (New York: Vintage Press, 1968), vol. 2, p. 6; *The Antichrist,* in *The Portable Nietzsche,* p. 62.

bureaucrats who blindly obey the will of history, as prisoners of language, as functions of a system. We surely are no mere rule-bound suburbanites. We are not compliant like Kafka's Joseph K., Veblen's technocrat, or B. F. Skinner's conditioned individual—and consequently withdraw from ironists who report on our victimization.

Feeling abused by one of Peter Handke's plays, *Offending the Audience* (1969), we part company with him. He overdoes it, claims too much, goes too far. His play subverts distinctions we need—distinctions between life and theater, off-stage necessity and on-stage freedom, beginnings and endings. It dissolves the line between play and reality, authors and their effects, nouns and verbs, nature and its manifestation, background truths and foreground untruths. His work offers no underlying positive view of the virtuous citizen or the good society, no view independent of what is enacted at the moment. All is appearance in a play which exploits the established theater only to deprive it of its limits. In his masterly survey, *The Antitheatrical Prejudice* (1981), Jonas Barish has reviewed what disconcerts us in Handke's presentation:

> *Offending the Audience* . . . confronts us with four actors, unnamed, wearing whatever they happened to be wearing, addressing us from an empty stage, in turn, according to no fixed rule. What they tell us, is that they have not come to present a play. They are not here to tell a story, to enact events, or to create a picture, not even a verbal picture. Nor are they about to engage in anything resembling impersonation. They will play no roles, not even the roles of themselves. Their assignment is merely to recite some words written for them by the author. The stage on which they stand is neither more nor less than what it appears to be, an unadorned platform. It contains neither entrances nor exits, nor are we being asked to imagine doors or windows (as in, for example, Thornton Wilder's *Our Town*). No other space is signified by the stage. It is simply a part of the building, lit just as the rest of the building is lit. Time is not, here, being represented either, any more than space or events. There is no imaginary time, no difference between time as lived by the audience and as experienced by the actors. It is possible indeed for the actors to claim that they are observing the classical unities, because of their refusal to split the theater into two halves. By speaking directly to the audience, without interruptions, intervals, pauses, or significant silences, they maintain a perfect unity of action.

> Nor, furthermore, do the stage figures wish to *express* anything, to arouse feeling in the audience, to involve them emotionally in grief or laughter. They will offer us no visual effects, no appeals to the senses or to the imagination. Nor will anything that happens on stage *signify* anything, as is usual in plays, where nonsense itself must mean something, and even "conspicuous meaninglessness" is designed to convey a meaning—where the action, whatever it may be, always points to some ulterior reality.[4]

Although Barish says that "nothing is being played," he implies that nothing *conventional* is being played, that because conventional forms have been rejected, *everything* is being played. The play is king. Handke and his players have so enlarged the arena for play that it is no longer possible to refer to its distinctive presence. Their action is staged to transform the nonactors who have appeared for no more than an evening in the theater. Handke treats the audience as if its members might yet, in his words, become the "playmakers and the counterplotters . . . the youthful comedians . . . the youthful lovers . . . the ingenues . . . the sentimentalists . . . the stars . . . the heroes and the villains of the piece."[5] Handke's performers shock and agitate their audience (much as Lenny Bruce used to savage his nightclub clientele) in order to extricate its members from their ordinary roles. Audiences, as Handke's actors make clear, have not discovered their capacity for action: they move without self-awareness. Their ultimate offense is that they believe in necessity—their own helplessness. They fail to see themselves as players—as playing victims. "Your playing," says one of Handke's actors to the audience, "was of exquisite nobility. . . . Play-acting was in your blood, you butchers, you buggers, you bullshitters, you bullies, you rabbits, you fuck-offs,

---

[4] Jonas Barish, *The Antitheatrical Prejudice* (Berkeley and Los Angeles: University of California Press, 1981), pp. 459–60. Barish shows how deeply players have disconcerted the Western world, how Plato, Augustine and the Church Fathers, the Jansenites, the Puritans, and Rousseau attacked the theater and the arts. Such anxiety is shared, for example, by Arthur C. Danto, who has noted how his own discipline of philosophy is subverted and trivialized when its products are treated as mere narratives, as mere performances (see his *The Philosophical Disenfranchisement of Art* [New York: Columbia University Press, 1986], especially pp. 136–61).

[5] Peter Handke, *Prosa Gedichte Theaterstuecke Hoerspiele Aufsaetze* (Frankfurt: Suhrkamp, 1969), pp. 199, 197–98.

you farts." You don't know it—you failed to assume responsibility for your parts—but you're nonetheless actors. "You troupers. You tear-jerkers. You potboilers. You foul mouths. You sell-outs. You dead-beats. You phonies. You milestones in the history of the theater."[6] Handke works to deprive the theater of its naturalism, its eagerness to duplicate a world in which individuals have become fixated by good sense, by their desire for security, cleanliness, efficiency, productivity, and utility. His actors abuse the audience not because it realistically enacts social roles but because it is so fully absorbed by the roles in which it has been cast. It is unaware of itself. Dismantling theatrical rituals in which audiences lose themselves, Handke reactivates the will to perform. He treats their compulsive behavior as a presentation; he regards *everything* one does as play. Treating self-presentations no less as acts for being shallow, frivolous, suicidal, habitual, trite, or autistic,[7] he provides the ground for a richer self by breaking the boundaries of both the encrusted self and an encrusted theater. However minimally, he moves toward irony, toward apprehending and accepting the world in all its apparent obtuseness. He pushes toward making everything indiscriminately present: "There are no two places here. Here there is but one place. . . . Here there is but *one* time."[8] He pushes toward total theater, ubiquitous play, postmodernist politics.

The offensiveness of the tactics of postmodernism is made evident by Push, the protagonist of Stanley Elkin's "A Poetic for Bullies." Push's credo is implicit in the very rush of Elkin's prose:

> I feel a power in me. I am Push, Push the bully, God of the Neighborhood, its incarnation of envy and jealousy and need. I vie, strive, emulate, compete, a contender in every event there is. I didn't make myself. I probably can't save myself, but maybe that's the only need I don't have. I taste my lack, and that's how I win—by having nothing to lose. It's not good enough! I want and I want and I will die wanting, but first I will have something. This time I will have something. I say it aloud. "This time I will have something." I step toward them. The power makes me dizzy. It is

---

[6] Ibid., pp. 209–10.

[7] R. D. Laing has defended this treatment for schizophrenic patients and Bruno Bettelheim for autistic children.

[8] Handke, *Prosa Gedichte Theaterstuecke Hoerspiele Aufsaetze,* pp. 197–98.

> enormous. They feel it. They back away. They crouch in the shadow of my outstretched wings. It isn't deceit this time but the real magic at last, the genuine thing: the cabala of my hate, of my irreconcilableness.[9]

"They back away," Push says, defining the costs of his onslaught. Departing from the conventions of the comfortable theaters of our ordinary lives, the ironist finds himself increasingly abandoned. He appears as mere assailant, an outsider who occupies a superior vantage point from which he presumes to know the parts others might play better than they do. If he does not temper his act, either his audience or his creator will strike back. In *Mansfield Park* Jane Austen depicts a character, Henry Crawford, for whom her very novel leaves no room. She portrays him as an idler who designs amateur theatricals for the sons and daughters of Mansfield Park while their responsible father is absent on a business trip. At one point Crawford says, "I really believe I could be fool enough at this moment to undertake any character that ever was written, from Shylock or Richard III down to the singing hero of a farce in his scarlet coat and cocked hat. I feel as if I could be anything or everything." Acting on his belief, he breaks up Mansfield Park, runs off in an adulterous elopement, and offends the very morality the novel supports. His mere presence offends Jane Austen, who uses him to define the virtues of society. Unredeemable, he is made to pay by being excluded.[10]

IT IS A price I paid as participant on a panel organized to entertain members of the Junior League at Honolulu's Kahala Hilton Hotel on "God or Guru—Have Times Really Changed?" Before lunch, we expounded for an hour. The next day the *Honolulu Star-Bulletin* reported the panel's effort to interest the hundred-odd assembled ladies:

> Bill Aulenbach, minister and coordinator for youth activities in Hawaii for the Episcopal Church; Mike Weinstein, assistant professor of sociology at the University of Hawaii; and Henry Kariel, professor of political science at the University were seated at the head table, vanda orchid leis draped

---

[9] Stanley Elkin, "A Poetic for Bullies," in *Criers & Kibitzers, Kibitzers & Criers* (New York: Random House, 1965), p. 206.

[10] Jane Austen, *Mansfield Park* (London: Macmillan, 1950), p. 123.

around their necks. Aulenbach allowed as how he didn't think times had changed at all, that "we all have our own god or guru," be it money, drugs, sex, or children. Weinstein talked about religion having a comeback on the college campus, "but not in its original form," citing yoga, transcendentalism, Erhard Seminar training.

And Kariel rammed it to the ladies.

He invited the women to look at themselves: "A couple of hours after breakfast, parking our cars, in the Waialae Room—consider the uniforms we wear, the faces we put on, our postures, how we are rigid and loose, the way we are—the way we are set in our ways."

A couple of women smiled, some turned to greet friends who had arrived at the gathering late, some looked at their fingernails or their neighbor's shoes. Others merely watched the elevators outside the room open to disgorge their passengers, hotel guests on their way to the beach. . . .

"See ourselves, see ourselves precisely, see where we are stuck," Kariel continued, "bored, caught, immobilized. See ourselves until we feel a vague urge to fidget, to cough, to look around, maybe, carefully, to move just a little. We are aching, aching to get out, quietly if we can manage it, certainly not wanting to make a fuss in the Waialae Room. . . . "

"Now, if you've played along with me—if you can imagine this really serious game continuing and becoming more intense . . . you may get some inkling of a concern for transcending the limitations of where you are now and move out of the present toward some richer life, something more fulfilling and exciting—or at least something less comfortable, straight, sensible, clean, well-mannered, and well-groomed, something less orderly and grammatic than my remarks. . . . "

Some women sat absorbed by Kariel's remarks. A few looked at their watches. "But where should you go?" Kariel continued, speaking out across the tastefully attired audience of young and middle-aged Junior Leaguers, Brahmins all. "And who should provide guidance? What of your churches? Those among us or those among the young who have come to perceive precisely where they are heading—nowhere really—might turn to the churches. . . . "

"The churches around you are eager to supply you with worthy causes, crusades, community projects, soul-saving missions. They are busy just when some of you have come to the edge and learned what your noble causes and crusades and projects have amounted to. . . . "

"Where, if we are bored by our comforts, if we want nothing grandiose, can we go? College courses in religion . . . mediation . . . some guru perhaps?

"There are adolescents among us who see the future and perceive its inanity, its emptiness, who may throw themselves away . . . become negligent, indifferent, vaguely suicidal—usually at the age of 11 or 12. They become sullen, uncommunicative. . . . Beyond their silence and their madness—if they do make it to the other side—they may touch on some holy realm of being, some other world, some transcendent order.

"But of course they'll not be able to tell us about it. There are no words to communicate with those they left behind, with those of us who are part of a sensible, well-ordered, well-dressed society. After all, we never felt that empty and useless and bored, at least not before two A.M. when the sleeping pill has begun to wear off. So we will organize panels, like this one, listen to speakers who say yes, everything's all right. God's in his heaven and in this world there is nothing worse, really, than Kent State, Attica, My Lai, Watergate, or perhaps a new vice president. And we will keep from feeling depressed by pushing our chairs around a bit (not making a fuss, certainly) . . . raising money for worthy charities . . . talking about gods and gurus and the young . . . then heading for the chef's salad in the Maile Room." A woman in the audience stood up to say that through religion we find meaning. Another woman said she was disturbed because she felt Kariel was "putting us down. You are sitting in judgment of us, of the Junior League."

The meeting was about over. One young woman leaned over to the woman sitting in front of her. "Heavy, heavy talk, wasn't it," she said, clapping as the panel was thanked for the coming. Another woman near the door politely tapped her hands together. "Me, I'm only clapping because it's over," she said to her relieved-looking neighbor. And the meeting was adjourned. On to lunch.[11]

And at lunch with a small group of the ladies, none of us could find a tactful way for retreating, for drawing the curtain. All too self-consciously we tested various kinds of polite silences until we returned to secure

---

[11] Barbara Morgan, "God, Guru, or the Chef's Salad?" *Honolulu Star-Bulletin*, September 27, 1979.

ground—our neighborhood, our language, the fortified institutions that keep us from panicking in the face of immoderate, tactless assaults on the meaning of our lives.

Ironical performances raise the most disconcerting of questions. Is not a life empty of purposes (beyond the one purpose of being playful) and free from morality (beyond the morality of consciousness-enhancing games) unbearably empty? What will happen to responsible conduct, good works, and high culture? Who will care to win gold stars in kindergarten, ribbons at the county fair, Nobel prizes? How will civilization be protected from fanatics who fail to play? Don't we need experts who are not playful, including experts in violence, so as to control people who are given to violence? Isn't less rather than more play necessary to cope with *real* destitution and suffering? Who would want priests, surgeons, teachers, soldiers, or bus drivers to be playful amateurs, to fiddle while Rome burns? Who would voluntarily give up the goods and services of a technological civilization? And should we not all share Arthur C. Danto's lament: "The age of pluralism is upon us. It does not matter any longer what you do, which is what pluralism means. When one direction is as good as another direction, there is no concept of direction any longer to apply."[12]

NO DOUBT THE relentless exposure of foundations will drive people beyond mere acts of withdrawal. Made to feel insecure, they will seek radical escapes from the discipline of enacting one's own lives. As Oscar Wilde was made to discover they will enact and enforce laws for relief from the freedom to define their own roles. Theirs becomes a movement in which opposites are extinguished and life is fulfilled. They behave as if trained in that Theater of Cruelty which Antonin Artaud designed to eliminate all hesitation in one's expressions. Accordingly, he kept his actors from playing roles by exhausting their resources for seeing themselves in action; he forced them to give their all. They were not to detach their laughs or screams from the feelings that give rise to them. His plays, he hoped, were "cruel" insofar as they would destroy the self-awareness of individuals who put on acts—whether they acted as members of his cast or his audience. The duplicity of irony would be overcome. Eliminating

[12] Danto, *The Philosophical Disenfranchisement of Art*, pp. 114–15.

public space for testing the viability of the diverse fragments constructed by the self, he subverted the theater—the human enterprise itself—at its very core. Inflamed by the madness of modern times, he seized that human arena in which consciousness of self and others is protected against the self-destructive consequences of either boredom or convulsion. He used and destroyed the space within which individuals can see themselves in action performing for their alter egos, for others. Although she focuses on Shakespeare's work, Helen Keyssar has implicitly defined the tension-charged space from which Artaud recoiled:

> When the world on the stage is maintained as separate from the world of the audience, we can be reminded fully of our separateness from the lives of others while simultaneously being confronted with the knowledge that we exist with others. My acknowledgement of Lear is different from Gloucester's or Lear's own self-acknowledgement simply because it is mine as much as Gloucester's is Gloucester's. But you do exist in a community with me as we sit side by side observing a performance. When you touch my hand or glance at me during a poignant moment it is not to say that we are made one (or five hundred) by that moment but that we are with each other. The confinement of the theater allows an intensification of the recognition of others, the revelation of knowledge of others' responses, but simultaneously emphasizes that we are not one but many.[13]

IT IS PRECISELY the unmediated, formless activism—the reverse of theatrical space—which Nietzsche attacked in his critique of Wagner's *Parsifal.* He contended that Wagner's operatic work had the effect of transfixing and unifying its audiences, that it created a state of overpowering excitements, "convulsions of 'moral' ecstasies."[14] He saw Wagner's spectacles as mind-killing hypnotic performances which revealed the power of the mass media—if not yet of Stalin's treason trials, Nazi party rallies. China's Cultural Revolution, Moral Majority crusades, or the engineered climaxes of American presidential politics.

---

[13] Helena Keyssar, "I Love You. Who Are You? The Strategy of Drama in Recognition Scenes," *PMLA* 92 (1977): 303.

[14] Friedrich Nietzsche, *Werke,* ed. Giorgio Colli and Massino Montinary (Berlin: de Gruyter, 1972), vol. 6, pp. iii, 417.

Yet Nietzsche refused to identify any alternative. No institution would do. He merely postulated a discipline to be mastered by a superhuman elite steeled to perform all possible roles without succumbing to any one. Only such an elite could hold its own against the self-aggrandizing demagogues at loose in the theaters of the politics of liberalism. Only the few could manage an ungrounded politics of play. Limiting politics to the few—"spiritualized Caesars"—who might master themselves, Nietzsche left an ominous vacuum which single-minded power seekers were to fill. They could universalize their private obsessions by annihilating whatever stood in the way. They could exploit the insecurities of the masses while dazzling intellectuals and artists by displays of sheer power.[15] A nonpolitical vision of society could become the property of fanatics like Hitler who, wholly apolitical, could impose their private obsessions and stop at nothing short of the peace of the grave. At the same time literary reactionaries like Knut Hamsen and Ezra Pound could rightly plead that they had been understood only in part, that the dictators of the day had turned out to lack the discipline for an inclusive politics.

Nietzsche would seem to have been alone in noting the futility of hectoring those who craved foundations and flocked to a savior. Unable to maintain their balance under pressure, the masses would but resent the kind of political process in which they themselves might become actors. Urging no crusade, Nietzsche offered only his own appearances—literary works which invite others to participate. Misunderstood as a manifesto for unmediated activism, his self-contradictory work—his flow of paradoxes, aphorisms, and questions—contributed to the very terror that irony seeks to forge into art. The failure to clear space for the participation of outsiders in one's own constructions it turns out, reduces the range of play and politics.

---

[15] See Fritz Stern, "Der Nationalsozialismus als Versuchung," in *Reflexionen Finsterer Zeit* (Tübingen: Mohr, 1984). Note also Benjamin Barber's comment: "The demand for superhuman capacities may permit ample human capacities to atrophy. The tendency of so many anarchists to end their careers of celebrating abstract man by reviling actual men is all but inevitable when the definition of *human* requires much more than most actual men have the strength to be. The cry that Nietzsche placed on Zarathustra's lips—'Man is something to be surpassed!'—leaves common women and men only with the despair of unachievable goals." (Benjamin Barber, *Strong Democracy* [Berkeley and Los Angeles: University of California Press, 1985], p. 82.)

8 PLAY AT THE END

THE postulate that history is relentlessly moving toward a global state which will be self-sustaining and self-ratifying, all-knowing and all-embracing has led me to join the most diverse of efforts to avoid going gently into that good night. Thus I have been consolidating a story that has been told in various languages, a story to which Alexis de Tocqueville contributed by projecting a future state that would quietly establish itself. Writing during the early part of the nineteenth century, mindful of the Terror of the French Revolution, he saw the United States on the way to becoming

> an immense, protective power which is alone responsible for securing their enjoyment and watching over their fate. That power is absolute, thoughtful of detail, orderly, provident, and gentle. It would resemble parental authority if, father-like, it tried to prepare its charges for a man's life, but on the contrary, it only tries to keep them in perpetual childhood. It likes to see the citizens enjoy themselves, provided that they think of nothing but enjoyment. It gladly works for their security, foresees and supplies their necessities, facilitates their pleasures, manages their principal concerns, directs their industry, makes rules for their testaments, and divides their inheri-

> tance. Why should it not entirely relieve them from the trouble of thinking and all the cares of living?
>
> Thus it daily makes the exercise of free choice less useful and rarer, restricts the activity of free will within a narrower compass, and little by little robs each citizen of the proper use of his own faculties.[1]

Shortly after 1900, Henry Adams wrote of the future as if it had already passed. "Power," he said, "leaped from every atom, and enough of it showed itself running to waste to supply the stellar universe at every pore of matter. Man could no longer hold it off. Forces grasped his wrists and flung him about as though he had hold of a live wire or a runaway automobile."[2] By 1945 J. Robert Oppenheimer, the wartime director of the Los Alamos Laboratory, could note that the productive process which yielded the first atomic bomb was "not only causal and determinate; it was objective in the sense that no human act or intervention qualified its behavior."[3]

Oppenheimer's conclusion, no less than Adams's or Tocqueville's, summarizes the melancholy sensibility of survivors who presume to see what remains obscure to others. Homeless and disenchanted, savoring every moment of consciousness, they experience apocalypse immanent in the present, death inhering in life. They perceive the present moment from a vantage point so extreme and so unnerving that it can scarcely be shared by others. For them, the future grows out of a present which provides no basis for action of *consequence,* for a politics of hope. They make light of groups that oppose the totalizing state, of mavericks and rebels who act in defiance of utilitarian calculations and computer printouts. Dismissing the movements of feminism, ecology, and ethnic minorities, they deny the possibility of a future state which tolerates space for marginality and difference, for play and politics.[4] They disallow Hannah Arendt's view

---

[1] Alexis de Tocqueville, *Democracy in America* (New York: Harper, 1966), pp. 666–67.

[2] Henry Adams, *The Education of Henry Adams* (Boston: Little Brown, 1918), p. 214.

[3] Quoted in Floyd Matson, *The Broken Image* (New York: Anchor Books, 1985), p. 3.

[4] For optimistic blueprints of postmodern society with multiple centers of resistance to the managerial state of capitalism, see Stanley Aronowitz, *The Crisis in Historical*

that "there are simply too many people in the world to make oblivion possible. One man will always be left alive to tell the story."[5]

To remain in action while accepting an irrevocable pessimism is to subscribe to the politics which disciplines the desperate maneuvers of postmodernism. Elaborately formulated by philosophers from Schiller to Dewey, this politics permeates activities to which I would wish to call attention—the reality-constructing practice of psychoanalysis, the meandering of ordinary conversation, the gyrations of feminist inquiry, and the self-reflective praxis of anthropological narratives. As the far more heated arts of postmodernism make clear, these activities, too, testify to a spirit of independence from the oppressive reality surrounding them—more precisely to a spirit which relates independence and dependence, detachment and involvement, indifference and affection. They engage in exercises of one-upmanship just short of dissolution. Experts in hype and make-believe—hyperbolists all—they outdistance a runaway technology while leaving themselves vulnerable to becoming its mindless accomplices. As they speed ahead they create structures which redeem society's trash and discards, the lost dimensions of experience. They recollect scattered fragments of our lives and forge them into wholes within which the dominant forces of modernity are crowded to the margin and become mere parts. They open space in which we can comprehend more of our lives. They induce us to experience more, to see and experience more fully.

WHETHER OR NOT she is categorized as artist, the postmodernist performer makes the most of the spaces between systems of power, using them not to create a new world but to make the most of the present one. She is the doctor who inserts her rambling asides and random thoughts in her professional diagnosis. She is the bridge player who takes note of the unnoticed parts of the game—the scraping of a chair, the extinction of a cigarette, the flicker of a smile. She is the anonymous designers of the 7-Up commercial which shows consumers refreshed in a ludicrous orgy beyond all possibilities of refreshment.

Postmodernists all, they resyncronize what has been previously

---

Materialism (New York: Praeger, 1981), and Roberto Mangabeira Unger, *Politics* (New York: Cambridge University Press, 1987).

[5] Hannah Arendt, *Eichmann in Jerusalem* (New York: Viking, 1983), p. 212.

synchronized—as in the lip-syncing antics of adolescents who reinforce the soundtrack. Even in an academic setting, they can feel on top of things by engaging in think-syncing:

> Sit prolongedly. At moments, abruptly leap up and pace the room, stare out a window, chew a pencil eraser, furrow the brow. Take deep, brain-oxygenating breaths; wince when a chain of hypothetical thought is broken by an imagined interruption. Do not shy from extending for days, even weeks, this exercise in participatory appreciation and vicarious achievement. At the end, feign scribbling on a piece of paper, or silently mouth with a contorted expression of triumph "*Cogito, ergo sum*" or "$E=mc^2$" or "Absolute power corrupts absolutely" or "*Le silence éternel de ces espaces infinis m'effraie.*"[6]

Giving energy to their abject resignation, those who follow such advice—it was given by John Updike—are like Bill Cosby, who in a TV commercial touted to children the virtues of Jell-O. They are no less like Richard Byrne, who trains executives to overcome their computerphobia, and on whose enthusiasm the *Los Angeles Times* reported in 1982:

> In January he and a colleague formed Springboard!, a firm to assist people to jump into the deep end of the communications revolution, enjoy the ride and come out surfing "the third wave."
>
> Another of Byrne's metaphors for this mastery is the trapeze act. "Ever seen a trapeze act?" he asks. "You've got to let go of one bar before you grab the next bar or it's not called a trapeze act. You've got to let go of the old paradigm and hang out in the void before you grab onto the new paradigm. In fact, the more uncertainty there is in between, the more not knowing, the more likely it is that you'll come up with a creative result. In a trapeze act, the longer you're in the void, the more money you get, the more satisfaction you create and the more risk you take. The void is where you've got to hang out as you move from one position to the next."
>
> Byrne has found that voids are not easy to negotiate when you're real comfortable in the old paradigm, when you're the lord and master of it as many of today's executives are.
>
> "I've noticed that many executives, particularly executives in high

---

[6] John Updike in "Talk of the Town," *New Yorker*, January 12, 1987, pp. 21–22.

technology companies, get nutty when you talk to them about personal computers," he reports. "A lot of executives are looking at retirement and they're wondering. 'Can I retire before I have to do this?' or they're thinking 'Maybe I could just die early.' "

And at a recent Springboard! training, executives not only sampled but instantly produced remarkable line, bar and pie-chart graphs depicting such things as the rise and fall of extraordinary love affairs. They created elaborate, six-month budget plans. They discovered how to use the computer as a personal clipping service. They checked out the news of a labor dispute by calling up a 20-minute-old UPI article on the subject. And they edited another UPI story, headlined, "Leftists Set Off Bombing Spree," to read "Leftists Set Off Kissing Spree." The computer automatically substituted the word "kiss" for the word "bomb" every time it appeared in the story.[7]

Such playing characterizes *all* efforts to outdistance the forces surrounding us. Anyone who copes with Otherness by adding to its dimensions demonstrates that, even though the world may be escape-proof, it remains possible to come to terms with the pressures it imposes. Not obliterated by technology, Max Weber could elaborate on the structure of bureaucracy, Norman Mailer on the technology of the moon shot, and Tom Wolfe on the regimen of astronauts and their families. Intensively in touch with heavy things of this world, they yet remained detached enough to treat them lightly. However close we may be to the end of enacting history, we have evidently not yet reached it. Although the future may be immanent within the present, contemporary structures of power certainly have not organized all perceptions. Adversarial cultures continue to cause trouble. We can still take comfort in the play of children who continue to play. Black and grey markets, shady ways of wheeling and dealing, are thriving. Love and anarchy remain beyond the range of a state whose monitors cannot record in what spirit we conform. And am I not in fact processing these words, still testing both my staying power and the firmness of the structures of reality that surround me?

Ahead of the momentum of modernity, beyond its present reach,

---

[7] Beth Ann Krier, "Specialist Helps Executives Get Over Their Fears of the New Technology," *Los Angeles Times,* August 11, 1982, pp. 18ff.

playgrounds remain for engaging in a form of politics wherein we can create more comprehensive structures. And within such structures, the roles of writer and reader, criminal and victim, teacher and student, doctor and patient are deconstructed and brought into new relationships. Within them, previously separate roles define one another and thereby constitute a theatrical world—an ever-shifting political order.

The strategy for extending the arena for theatricality has been summarized by Hubert Dreyfus. First one must break up ("deconstruct," he says) theoretical abstractions while demonstrating that "human beings and the objects they encounter are formed by cultural practices." The first step, in other words, is to show that seemingly invariable institutions depend on the variable actions of human beings.

> Second, one must give an interpretation of our current cultural situation by finding a cultural paradigm (for Heidegger, the hydroelectric power station on the Rhine; for Foucault, the prison), which focuses our dominant practices, while at the same time assembling all the evidence in our micro-practices—and this of course includes our linguistic practices—that an alternative understanding of human beings once existed and still continues, although drowned out by our everyday busy concerns. Finally, having done this job, one can only hope that the micro-practices excluded by technology will find a new focus in a new paradigm.[8]

What this strategy entails is apparent not only in the arts. Within the technicism of modernity there are myriad pursuits which reveal the promise of deep play. To focus on these is to perceive the potential for extending postmodernism's engagement with technology—that is, for using whatever resources we have for enacting more of our collective selves. A log of mine reveals possibilities:

> After Wayne Fiedler said he would tolerate any embarrassment I might create in his political science class, he introduced me as a guest lecturer. His class had read and discussed an article of mine. I moved behind the desk, sat down, leaned slightly forward, looked expectant, and said nothing. I of-

---

[8] Hubert L. Dreyfus, "Holism and Hermeneutics," *Review of Metaphysics* 34 (September 1980): 3–23.

fered a slight smile and noted a few smiles from several students. An air of anticipation while nothing happened. While silence stretched beyond convention toward embarrassment, I was glad Wayne did not break his promise to bear with me. I leaned forward a bit more as if to say "Well?" Heads turned away, eyes were shielded. Out of the silence came a rasping cough, which was quickly covered by a cough from the back, as if echoed. The first cough was repeated. I thought of two drummers in the jungle, realizing I must have missed previous smaller gestures, an array of less audible efforts to communicate. Someone moved his chair, scraping it. I moved a bit backwards. One student opened a newspaper at the very moment that another started to read the book she had in front of her. *Only four minutes had elapsed.*

Two boys began to whisper with one another. The girl who had started to read wrote a note and passed it to her neighbor. I was dying to know what it said and did not mind looking curious. The note was passed on, read by another girl, and returned with a knowing smile. Smiles suddenly lit up this small group. Several communities had emerged during my mute presence: two coughers, several chair movers, two boys, a group of three note-readers. Four groups had transcended reticence and made their appearance.

On my right, an older student now grinned broadly, his eyes very open. "I guess," he started slowly, "you're wondering what sort of questions we have after discussing your article." I looked at him encouragingly. He continued: "You wrote something about the way. . . . " He went on and reviewed what he thought I wrote, ending with a question about it. Everyone was grateful now and focused on me. I offered no relief. The same student came to everyone's aid: "I guess when you wrote that, you must have meant. . . . " And he went on to explain what he thought I must have meant, looking at me, asking for confirmation. At this point, I felt ready to confirm anything, but there was no need because another student proceeded: "That wasn't meant at all. What he really meant. . . . "

A total of nine minutes had passed, and a miracle of sorts had occurred: I was de-authorized and two people actually began a discussion and others listened. In a setting in which the alternatives to communication were anger or boredom or anxiety or self-absorption, people had begun to relate. It wasn't much of a discussion—but it was certainly theirs.

> For me it only remained to keep the situation from seeming weird, to make quite explicit that it was no accident at all. Accordingly, I now broke in and reviewed what I though I saw and heard. I asked others to give their account of what had transpired. It had become easy now for us to take note of the conditions under which communities might be formed, of who leads and who follows, of the charisma of founding fathers, of the relationship between sex, authority, age, and participation, of the segregation of latecomers, of the prerequisites for political development, of the structure of government, of the shifting ground of politics. Not quite holding the mirror up to the class, I was yet aware of an infinity of reflections—even as at the end I still gave weight to the safe concepts of political science and betrayed my commitment to the prevailing play of forces.

WERE A CLASS of students—any organization—treated as a function of the continuous desire to transform its boundaries, it would be devoid of a durable subject at its center. Because everything at its margin would qualify for integration, it would be continuously testing its capacity for including the forces impinging on it. Thus the meaning of its subject matter would remain open until the class had run its course, until it had been grounded. Its specific content, like the content of conversation, would be as various as the rules for bringing unacknowledged dimensions of experience into play. At its best, it would displace that form of inquiry which is designed to eliminate error and reveal truth while it would extend one's knowledge of oneself and of others.[9]

Unlike forms of inquiry designed to get to the bottom of things and put doubts to rest, conversation allows its members to relish categorical overflow, a surplus of meaning, a freedom from what goes as evidence. Whereas inquiry is blocked by false leads, conversation thrives on them.

---

[9] In *Chan is Missing* (1984), Wayne Chang dramatizes the differences between gaining knowledge by focused inquiry and by playful cruising. Two cabdrivers from San Francisco's Chinatown are searching for a cabdriver named Chan who had absconded with the funds of one of them. Proceeding like Edgar Allan Poe's detective in "The Purloined Letter," they cruise through Chinatown quite contrary to the deductive method featured in Charlie Chan movies. In the process, they (and the audience) gain increasingly complex knowledge of their past, of one another, of their community, and of the missing Chan. In the end, Chan has become increasingly meaningful though he remains missing.

It departs from the view of the mind as an objective tribunal in which beliefs are cross-examined and conclusions reached. Whenever a conversation does result in some conclusion, as Michael Oakeshott has noted, "thoughts of different species take wing and play around one another, responding to each other's movements and provoking one another to fresh exertion."[10] Points that are made are superseded by an irrelevant remark until, at best, illustrations fail to illustrate, the literal reference is transformed by the figurative. Full of bypasses, conversation is guided by unembarrassed curiosity—the gossip's eagerness to hear what happened next, what happened before. It ends only when its participants withdraw or retire, when, bored or fatigued, they tire out. And even then it goes on in the form of internal dialogues as one keeps on reflecting, turning parts of it over in one's mind, thinking of what one might have said, adding embarrassing notions, making indiscreet remarks, remaining stimulated and sleepless. Behind those words, Walt Whitman sings:

> I have heard what the talkers were talking, the talk of the
> beginning and the end.
> But I do not talk of the beginning or the end.

Conversation is necessarily ecological, for precisely what lies at the edge of one's field of vision, on the tip of one's tongue, or at the margin of one's consciousness is introduced and symbolized. New subjects come to be embraced lightly enough so that they might be relinquished. Introduced not to make a point but to keep conversation alive, they are abandoned when they threaten the conversational process itself, when they have become either so pointed, indiscreet, or tactless that they alienate the participants.

Unlike inquiring, conversing is a flirtatious activity that evades all endings, including its own. In Wallace Stevens's characterization, it is

> the merely going round,
> Until the merely going round is a final good,
> The way wine comes at a table in a wood.

---

[10] Michael Oakeshott, *Rationalism in Politics* (New York: Basic Books, 1962), p. 198. See also Georg Simmel, *The Sociology of Georg Simmel* (New York: Free Press, 1950), pp. 50–53.

One feels good as it goes on—and better as it goes on ever more intricately, inviting ever more distinctions, leading to ever greater refinements. Like Eros flirting, it builds suspense by the deferral of ultimate meaning. The tensions it thereby engenders are those inherent in the psychoanalytical process in which unacknowledged experiences of one's life are related in ever greater depth, in which relationships are extended.

Freud, it is true, found it necessary to distinguish his practice from conversation. He addressed a hypothetical patient and issued a warning:

> Your talk with me must differ in one respect from an ordinary conversation. Whereas usually you rightly try to keep the threads of your story together and to exclude all intruding associations and side-issues, so as not to wander too far from the point, here you must proceed differently. You will notice that as you relate things various ideas will occur to you which you feel inclined to put aside with certain criticisms and objections. You will be tempted to say to yourself: "This or that has no connection here, or it is quite unimportant, or it is nonsensical, so it cannot be necessary to mention it." Never give in to these objections.[11]

Freud felt that a conversation could not accommodate what is "quite unimportant or nonsensical." He saw it narrowly as a guarded exchange, perhaps as characteristic of the Vienna of his day. Determined to deprive expressions of their point, he designed a procedure which encourages narration to be indiscreet, people to mince no words, to say what comes to mind, and to welcome "asides" which are ordinarily dismissed as being beside the point. Asides especially are to be related to impel the patient's recognition of the larger, downright mythological dimension of her effort to formulate a usable past. If, then, she feels increasingly composed, this is because what had been put out of mind had emerged—or rather was *made* to emerge by agonizing analytic work. Encouraged by the analyst, she seeks to make a coherent whole out of a welter of repressed fragments. She works in a setting that includes an analyst who will not correct or dismiss, a setting in which so-called facts have no weight, in which all that matters is how effectively her narrative works to unblock the channels for

---

[11] Sigmund Freud, "On the Beginning of the Treatment" (1913), in Ernest Jones, ed., *Collected Papers* (London: Hogarth Press, 1949), p. 355.

communication, to free her from reticence, approved good manners, censored speech, private thoughts. On the minimal stage defined by Freud, she is expected to stumble across troublesome events, betray them by denying their significance, by slips of her tongue, by "accidental" gestures. And in her very effort to identify them she will associate them with one another, establish their connection, make them cohere. In the process of composing, she will become composed.

An American analyst, Stuart Schneiderman, has perceived the theatrical quality of the psychoanalytical process by placing it at the center of Jacques Lacan's practice:

> Nothing real happens in a psychoanalysis; the real must always remain outside. Perhaps because Lacan was hysterical and histrionic, he saw analysis as akin to theater. Its base and foundation are to be found in a specific theatrical genre, which I will call high comedy. It is rare indeed that an analysand will see things this way; analysands usually have other genres in mind. Anything but comedy, for comedy lacks seriousness and most analysands want above all to be taken seriously.[12]

Freud, it need hardly be said, wanted to be taken seriously, just as he wanted the patient to take herself seriously. But he insisted that "the opposite of play is not what is serious but what is real."[13] He knew the dangers of grounding the analytical process in a projected "reality": analysis itself led patients to cling to the analyst, to become lovesick and stop doing the work of free association. Calling it "transference," he knew that it was something other than "the charms of my person" that led to their attachment to him and finally to *all* the realities human beings construct. "We overcome the transference," Freud hoped, "by pointing out to the patient that his feelings do not arise from the present situation and do not apply to the person of the doctor, but that he is repeating something that happened to him earlier."[14] Of course, it would be hard for

---

[12] Stuart Schneiderman, *Jacques Lacan* (Cambridge: Harvard University Press, 1983), p. 37.

[13] Sigmund Freud, "Creative Writers and Daydreaming," *Standard Edition* (London: Hogarth Press, 1959), vol. 9, p. 144.

[14] Sigmund Freud, *Introductory Lectures* (1917).

analysts to remain nondirective. Given the analyst's extended presence in the life of the patient, it would be odd were he not perceived as playing a commanding role, one that counsels some specific course of action, and thereby terminates analysis. Analysts make self-referential comments; even their silences vary and instruct. Reality enters the consulting room and grounds the patient's performance.[15] Yet there are exemplary analysts. Thus for Stuart Schneiderman, Lacan was "a creature from another planet" who usually succeeded—often near hysteria—in keeping reality at bay, in making the patient emerge as the sole performer:

> Free association dispenses with the logical connectives of neurotic discourse and attempts to discover another logic. For Lacan this new construction was something that emerged during the course of the analysis; it was rare that he himself made connections or constructions. Basically he waited for the patient to be able to connect things up for himself. And since during the course of analysis these connections were usually those of the neurosis, Lacan would content himself with signifying that such an interpretation was not right. Generally he let things slide as long as he could. He did not conceptualize his role as that of the interpreter, offering meanings for each dream and symptom. The tremendous intelligence we read in his writings was not something that he bandied about very often in sessions. The burden of interpreting as a regular, even a daily activity passed into the hands of the analysand. And as long as this activity was proceeding, which meant that the patient was offering different interpretations, Lacan let things move along at their own pace. His interpretations were limited to those occasions where the patient reached a point of certainty and conviction that caused the dialogue to stop.
>
> Lacan as an analyst was not trying to establish any sort of communication with his patients; nor did he think it a good idea that they understand each other. Like most analysts he encouraged free association but did not listen to it as if it were the ranting of someone involved in a gratuitous sort of self-indulgence. Lacan, like most analysts, listened as if the remarks that were about him were really addressed to someone else and as if the remarks

---

[15] Sigmund Freud, *Analysis of Transference* (New York: International Universities Press, 1982.) See also Adolf Grunbaum, *The Foundations of Psychoanalysis: A Philosophical Critique* (Berkeley and Los Angeles: University of California Press, 1984.)

> of the analysand that were supposed to be about himself were really about an other. This he did without saying very much. By acting much of the time as if he were a creature from another planet, even another galaxy, Lacan gave the impression that he was hearing something other than what you were saying. He never put himself on the same wavelength as his analysand, but remained always at cross purposes. He never tried to find areas of agreement and accord, but scrupulously maintained a fruitful, well-tuned discord.[16]

To promote the patient's reenactment of a repressed past, Lacan worked to maintain an arena cleared of his imposing presence. No models except the patient's own were to show the way. The patient himself would have to populate the stage, to give form to whatever reality pressed itself on his consciousness. He would have to keep changing roles and rules to cope with the ever-changing threats to his playground. Ceasing to do good, he would become an actor.

Deft and shifty, forever dissembling, the discipline of such an individual would be hard to take. Others who have firmer principles rightly suspect that for him integrity is merely a capacity for coming to terms with the unnamed elements of man's fate. Analyst or patient—there is finally no distinction—he cares only about the coming-to-terms process itself, which he views aesthetically, not morally. Acting in morally neutral space, he manifests what Immanuel Kant called man's aesthetic function; but unlike Kant, he is indifferent to everything else. He is playful, nothing more.

SHORTLY AFTER KANT elaborated on his conception of aesthetics in the *Critique of Judgment,* Friedrich Schiller relied on it to develop a view of art as sheer medium through which we move from a sensuous to a conscious state of existence. In his *Letters on the Aesthetic Education of Man* (1793–1795), Schiller treated play as the concrete embodiment of Kant's aesthetics. Sensuous experience and formalistic abstraction, Schiller said, are united in play; play harmonizes necessity and freedom, the tyranny of the senses and the tyranny of reason. Within the process of play

---

[16] Schneiderman, *Jacques Lacan,* pp. 118–19.

unrepressed sensuousness and repressive rationality are related. In an unbalanced instrumentalist culture guided by a utilitarian rationality, play holds the promise of reintegrating man. In an increasingly industrialized society, so Schiller argued before the concept of alienation became a cliché, "enjoyment is separated from labor, the means from the end, exertion from recompense. Eternally fettered only to a single little fragment of the whole, man fashions himself only as a fragment; ever hearing only the monotonous whirl of the wheel which he turns, he never develops the harmony of his being, and, instead of shaping the humanity that lies in his nature, he becomes a mere imprint of his occupation, his science."[17] To integrate rationality and sensuousness in the face of technology requires making sensuousness rational and rationality sensuous. When the play impulse, as Schiller called it, is followed, we cease to be *governed* by either sensuousness or rationality. Engaging both, idling between them, we become composed—but reach no final state which defines our being. Sensuousness, Schiller maintained, must be brought into play where it can engage the oppressive forces of a technique-centered society. To be sure, the expression of sensuousness—of libidinal forces—is no less to be feared than the triumph of rationality. But *in play restraints emerge in the very process in which sensuousness finds expression.* Expressed in the midst of a community of fellow players, feelings are shaped and directed rather than simply released.[18]

More than a century after Schiller reacted to a still embryonic industrialism by writing of the promise of play, Hannah Arendt responded to the forces of totalitarianism—specifically to the passions unleashed by the way Nazism used technology to systematize the rest of Europe's intermittent anti-Semitism. Most basically she condemned Nazism's rejection of politics, its ruthless exclusiveness, its determination to annihilate Otherness rather than to integrate it. Her very metaphors bring the play impulse into relation with politics, for they make it possible to see total-

---

[17] Friedrich Schiller, *The Aesthetic Letters,* trans. J. Weiss (Boston: Little Brown, 1945), p. 22.

[18] See ibid., pp. 63, 145. In Schiller's judgment, the emerging technology would fail to display itself; it would simple be *there,* a force which expresses nothing—which was being *made* to express nothing beyond its own momentum.

itarian regimes as wholly opposed to theater, the Nazi party rallies as nonperformances, Hitler as nonactor. For her, politics and play require the presence of others: "Performing artists—dancers, play-actors, musicians, and the like—need an audience to show their virtuosity just as acting men need the presence of others before whom they can appear; both need a publicly organized space for the performance itself. . . . The Greek polis once was precisely that "form of government" which provided men with a space of appearances where they could act, with a kind of theater." Arendt recalled that for the ideal politician—she singled out Jefferson—the esteem of his fellow actors was of higher value than anything else.[19]

EXTENDING THE JEFFERSONIAN ideal, John Dewey was to argue for an equally noninstrumental conception of democratic politics, seeing it not as means that would lead to some ultimate good but as intrinsically good. He characterized democratic politics as an experimental process in which participants continuously take risks to come to terms with novel experience. Implicated in such praxis, we learn to act, he wrote, by acting, to play by playing: play alone is king. There is but one authentic community, one Richard Rorty identifies with pragmatism: "Our identification with our community—our society, our political tradition, our intellectual heritage—is heightened when we see this community as ours rather than nature's, shaped rather than found, one among many which men have made. In the end, the pragmatists tell us, what matters is our loyalty to other human beings clinging together against the dark, not our hope of getting things right."[20]

Such pragmatism defines the concerns of feminist movements which have begun to desublimate the conventional hierarchy of command, division of labor, organization of the household, and priorities of sex. More than assaulting the off-limits signs posted at the boundary of the private sector, they are subverting the dominant idea of growth and education by insisting on a form of praxis which denies that we must first learn and then

---

[19] Hannah Arendt, *On Revolution* (New York: Viking Press, 1963), pp. 127, 259.

[20] Richard Rorty, "Pragmatism, Relativism, and Irrationalism," in *Proceedings and Addresses of the American Philosophical Association* 53 (1980): 727.

do, first gain theoretical knowledge and then engage in action. Among feminists, Mary Daly in particular has been firming up the idea that we learn to enact our lives not by following a linear path but by moving in an expanding upward spiral. Sporting a mixed metaphor, she regards the spider's web as a spiral: "Genuine spinning is spiraling, which takes us over, under, around the baffle gates of godfathers into the Background." And the background remains undefined, for it is a value-neutral, aesthetic space, its substance free from the venerable distinctions of natural-unnatural, mind-body, doctor-patient, male-female, success-failure, private-public, discrete-indiscrete, life-death, means-ends, theory-practice. What emerges within this space is wholly contingent on the ever-variable interests which are brought under conscious control in conversation, in spinning tales:

> Spinsters spin and weave, mending and creating unity of consciousness. In doing so we spin through and beyond the realm of multiple split consciousness. In concealed workshops, Spinsters unsnarl, unknot, untie, unweave. We knit, knot, interlace, entwine, whirl, and twirl. Absorbed in Spinning, in the ludic cerebration which is both work and play, Spinsters span the dichotomies of false consciousness and break its mind-binding combinations.[21]

Mary Daly's project finds its echo in the writing of Kostas Axelos, who interprets Marx's praxis as an effort to displace what is assumed to be Truth. He would deploy Truth by treating it interchangeably as the truth central to error and as the error central to truth. Because of the equivocal character of all human formulations, of whatever appears in the world, he maintains that we can only engage in transactions between truth and

---

[21] Mary Daly, *Gyn-Ecology: The Metaethics of Radical Feminism* (Boston: Beacon Press, 1978), pp. 405, 386. Edgar Allan Poe maintained that such play is the distinctive attribute of human beings: "Diddling—or the abstract idea conveyed by the verb to diddle—is sufficiently well understood. Yet the fact, the deed, the thing, *diddling,* is somewhat difficult to define. We may get, however, at a tolerably distinct conception of the matter at hand, by defining—not the thing, diddling, in itself—but man, as an animal that diddles. . . . Man is an animal that diddles, and there is *no* animal that diddles *but* man." ("Diddling: Considered as One of the Exact Sciences," in *The Works of Edgar Allan Poe* [New York: Plymouth Publishing Co., n.d.], pp. 128–29, courtesy of Robert S. Cahill].)

error. Such transactions are but play. They are the process of *endlessly* relating polarized extremities. And such relating is necessarily "without a point of view, without one-sided direction (neither spiritualistic nor idealistic or materialistic nor realistic)." It is an overarching, "planetary" activity—not a final being, to be sure, but a "being-in-becoming of the totality of the world," a being in revolution which he simply calls play. Within play, there is neither truth nor its opposite:

> Planetary thought answers to the errance of the being-in-becoming of the totality of the world. What, then, happens to truth? Errance does not mean error and aberration, falsity, vagrancy, and lying. There is no longer any reference to an absolute—something absolved from what?—but just the play of "It." Everything does not become relative—relative to what?—but constitutes an approach to "It," to the ungraspable, which is neither an idea, nor a person, nor a thing. It "is" the play of time which does not allow stabilizing being, hypostasizing becoming, positing totality, and taking the world as a supposition. . . . Truth . . . becomes question, problem, interrogation, in the play of errance. . . . Reality becomes itself question, problem, interrogation, and even play. . . . What is to be done? *Play the play.* Let ourselves be carried by the play of time which is—at the same time?—movment and rest, concentration and dispersal, gathering and shattering.[22]

To this prescription Axelos adds that insofar as technology encircles us and forges everything, insofar as it is the all-embracing instrument in the struggle between us and our environment, we have no choice but fully to participate in it.[23] Technology must be thought, experienced, and performed. If it obliterates boundaries, eradicates distinctions, deconstructs structures, and blends genres, we ouselves must simply get involved in more of it, naming it more elaborately than we name the planets, the hurricanes, and weapon systems that, when not *played,* surround and terrorize us. To survive, we must universalize play.

What is entailed by universalizing play is shown by Clifford Geertz's

---

[22] Cited in Kostas Axelos, *Alienation, Praxis, and Techne in the Thought of Karl Marx* (Austin: University of Texas Press, 1976), p. 342 (my emphasis).

[23] See Kostas Axelos, *Einführung in ein künftiges Denken* (Tübingen: Max Niemeyer, 1966), pp. 27–42.

reconstruction of the society of nineteenth-century Bali. In his exuberant interpretation, Bali's culture was wholly expressive. All activities were regarded as instrumental embellishments; all were regarded as appearances; all were dramatized. Nor was drama a mere facade to assure the effectiveness of government:

> The expressive nature of the Balinese state was apparent through the whole of its known history, for it was always pointed not toward tyranny, whose systematic concentration of power it was incompetent to effect, and not even very methodically toward government, which it pursued indifferently and hesitantly, but rather toward spectacle, toward ceremony, toward the public dramatization of the ruling obsessions of Balinese culture: social inequality and status pride. It was a theatre state in which the kings and princes were the impresarios, the priests the directors, and the peasants the supporting cast, stage crew, and audience. The stupendous cremations, tooth filings, temple dedications, pilgrimages, and blood sacrifices, mobilizing hundreds and even thousands of people and great quantities of wealth, were not means to political ends: they were the ends themselves, they were what the state was for. Court ceremonialism was the driving force of court politics; and mass ritual was not a device to shore up the state, but rather the state, even in its final gasp, was a device for the enactment of mass ritual. Power served pomp, not pomp power.

Geertz's account of Balinese performances are not a facade behind which reality unfolds and law is enforced. Thus the politics of Bali is contrary to that of the West, where presidential inaugurations and state funerals—not to mention Hitler's party rallies—are treated as theatrical techniques for mobilizing and integrating diverse interests for the pursuit of specific goals. In the West, the *play* of politics is seen as instrument to mystify the population and produce compliance. Ceremonies are designed to entrap the population: they are but trappings to legitimate the jockeying for power. The Western state's semiotic aspects, Geertz writes, "exaggerate might, conceal exploitation, inflate authority, or moralize procedure." To reduce Bali's politics to this Western view, according to Geertz, would be to fail to see "the poetics of power."[24]

---

[24] Clifford Geertz, *Negara: The Theatre State in Nineteenth-Century Bali* (Princeton: Princeton University Press, 1980), pp. 13, 123, 135.

The West may find it easier to see how fully reality may be transformed by interpreting the culture of Japan as creatively—as artfully—as Geertz has interpreted that of Bali. Japan may be seen not only to imitate what is imposed on it but also to bring imitation to such a high pitch that nothing remains but an aesthetics—the poetry of power. In *The Empire of Signs* (1970), Roland Barthes noted that "[Tokyo] does possess a center, but this center is empty. The entire city turns around a site both forbidden and indifferent, a residence concealed beneath foliage, protected by moats, inhabited by an emperor who is never seen, which is to say, by no one knows who." Nothing identifiable as distinctively Japanese would seem to ground either its people or its artifacts. The Japanese quest for self-definition—for what it means to be Japanese—is an unending one. Donald Richie, an author of books on Noh plays and Japanese cinema who has lived for many years in Tokyo, points to the center of this preoccupation:

> Appearance *is* the reality here. The ostensible is the real. . . . No matter how hard you look, the mask *is* the face. There is no notion of "the real me," a being somehow separate from the person. People here are what you can see, constructed from the outside. The Japanese take what is well known and emblematic in the West and *own* it. And it's not a question of their being "plastic" people, because everything here is "plastic". . . . *Everything* here is presentational.[25]

The truth disappears behind Japanese conversations and negotiations in which participants say the opposite of what they mean while aware of their duplicity. Brute frankness emerges only near the loss of consciousness—as when men keep drinking and the discipline which maintains the ironies of Japanese life collapses.[26] Sober and alert, they balance life's opposites. They sustain the heady eclecticism associated with post-

---

25 Donald Richie, quoted in Christopher Lasch, *The Minimal Self* (New York: W. W. Norton, 1984), p. 146.

26 See John David Morley, *Pictures from the Water Trade: Adventures of a Westerner in Japan* (Boston: Atlantic Monthly Press, 1985), especially Morley's account of Japanese eroticism, its ceaseless titillation lest the reality of fulfillment end the process. Morley also refers to the work of Maruyama Masao, a political philosopher who has noted how the depth of Japan's eclecticism, its life in contradiction, its indifference to any settled foundation, baffles Westerners who have different notions of integrity and trust.

modernist architecture which, as Richie has observed, is "a glorious architectural confusion of Corinthian columns and chromium pylons, dormer windows and curved escalators, half-timber, plain red brick, sheet steel, textured lucite."[27] Why, he asks, have the Japanese bothered to franchise a Disneyland in their suburbs? In Clifford Geertz's Bali and Donald Richie's Japan, the ostensible is real, the mask is the face. Nothing is privileged as foreground is reduced to background. Everything is presentational—is present.

SUCH A STATE is not unfamiliar to us. At one time or another we have all exchanged a wide-eyed look of recognition, a look so comprehensive that it is all equalizing. However briefly, it passes between hunter and prey, doctor and patient, mother and child. Filled with that acknowledgment of the other, it is neither defensive nor offensive. Wholly disarming, it generates a relationship that has no purpose beyond its being. We have no agenda for the future. For the moment, we are lovers who have dispelled reality: *every* appearance is all right.

That such a state of intense purposelessness is not out of our reach is shown by Richard Rush's *Stunt Man* (1980), a quite conventional film which dramatizes the drama of passage from terror to composure. Lucky Cameron (Steve Railsback) is led out of the intractable world of reality when he joins a company of actors engaged in making a mawkish World War I movie. Under the direction of Eli Cross (Peter O'Toole), who commands the sun to shine so that the cameras can roll, all those assembled on and off the movie set create an ephemeral world of make-believe—a world quite other than the dreadfully real one Cameron had been frantically seeking to escape. Cameron is not only a recent veteran of the Vietnam War and a broken marriage; he is also on the run from the police, whom he eludes by stumbling into the movie set, where Cross appreciates his desperate energy, adopts him, and leads him toward becoming an all-accepting performer. Cameron is afraid he won't be able to deceive the pursuing police, but Cross reassures him: "You'll be disguised as a stunt man who doubles for an actor who plays an American flier who

---

[27] See Donald Richie, in Mildred Friedman, ed., *Tokyo: Form and Spirit* (New York: Abrams, 1986).

poses as a German soldier who, like yourself, is a fugitive." Confused by Cross's way of continuously redefining everyone's expectations, paranoid and frightened, Cameron nevertheless learns to keep his balance with the help of a motherly coach. Passing increasingly difficult tests, he is slowly drawn into realizing that nothing is real, that attachments may be dead-serious and yet do not matter. At the end, the leading lady with whom he has fallen in love suddenly deserts him. When she returns, all would seem to be happily resolved. Yet there is no Happy Ending, for she unaccountably runs off again—and gives the audience a chance to see Cameron, who near his breaking point, breaks into a grin and then laughs wholeheartedly: it's all an act, *and all of it all right*—the death of the stuntman he's replaced, the ruptures in relationships he's experienced, the reversals of plotted continuity. He's been near death in Vietnam, near madness and murderous jealousy back home, near panic on the movie set. Nothing more can happen to him. He's made the transition, earned his laugh. No longer fleeing reality, he embraces it as unreal. He has undergone a discipline, a therapeutic testing of self that moved him toward an awareness of the transitoriness of all commitments.

The film, I don't mind acknowledging, certainly demands little of its audience: when ominous smoke erupts from Eli Cross's helicopter, it all too quickly turns into streams of color; when actors are shown to have suffered from a sickening accidental bombardment, their wounds are shortly revealed to be a cosmetic triumph. We aren't deeply touched. Yet for a moment we are prompted to realize that we might learn to accept that interpretations of events are endless, that meanings depend on contexts, that nothing whatever is certain.

If we ourselves cannot act within this narrative of light-spirited survival this is obviously because we are not sufficiently drawn into it. In a world in whose dramas we do not actively participate, it transforms us no more than stories such as the one told about Ch'ing Yaun who, after thirty years of Zen study, arrived in an undifferentiated continuum of nihilism in which nothing is required and everything is permitted. Before his study, it is said, he had made familiar, home-grown distinctions. Evil had been evil and goodness had been goodness. He had seen mountains as mountains and waters as waters. After his course of study, however, he arrived at greater knowledge and saw that mountains were not mountains and waters not waters. It is as if he had passed a disruptive introductory course and come to realize that things were no longer what they seemed to be. But instead of staying with this hard-won nihilism, Ch'ing Yaun studied thirty more years and finally reached the incommunicable heart of Zen where it was all right for anything to be anything. He became free to see mountains as mountains and waters as waters, although his new way of being was not what it had been in the beginning. Now he smiled as he honored neither the labels he attached to nature nor an unlabeled nature—only the poet's brush which maintains the unresolved tension between them.

At the end, Ch'ing Yaun's life is as intense as it is devoid of resolutions. Having survived confinement and paranoia, having gyrated through increasingly trying experiences, having abandoned his hardened self, he finds himself in space cleared for eroticizing the polarized antinomies of existence. Like puns and aphorisms, he emerges as shifty, open-ended, and meaning-dispersing. There is no telling what his words really mean. He is as pervasively equivocal as the careers of weightless, ungrounded orphans and Doppelgänger, as actors whom Nietzsche idealized as supermen.

To use the male pronoun, as I have been, is to ignore the case for moving toward inconclusiveness that has been appropriated by the discourse of feminism. Thus Luce Irigaray, a French feminist who has been most influential among literary and film critics, maneuvers past masculine parameters for conceptualizing reality. The "geography of pleasure," she writes, is such that it cannot be comprehended by the dominant imagery. A "phallic economy" cannot grasp that "women have sex organs more or less everywhere." Irigaray addresses men—or rather the discourse of masculinity:

> "She" is indefinitely other in herself. This is doubtless why she is said to be whimsical, incomprehensible, agitated, capricious . . . not to mention her language, in which "she" sets off in all directions leaving "him" unable to discern the coherence of any meaning. Hers are contradictory words, somewhat made from the standpoint of reason, inaudible for whoever listens to them with ready-made grids, with a fully elaborated code in hand. For in what she says, too, at least when she dares, woman is constantly touching herself. She steps ever so slightly aside from herself with a mur-

mur, an exclamation, a whisper, a sentence left unfinished. . . . When she returns, it is to set off again from elsewhere. From another point of pleasure, or of pain. One would have to listen with another ear, as if hearing *an "other meaning" always in the process of weaving itself, of embracing itself with words, but also of getting rid of words in order not to become fixed, congealed in them.* For if "she" says something, it is not, it is already no longer, identical with what she means. . . .

It is useless, then, to trap women in the exact definition of what they mean, to make them repeat (themselves) so that it will be clear; they are already elsewhere in that discursive machinery where you expected to surprise them. They have returned within themselves. Which must not be understood in the same way as within yourself. They do not have the interiority that you have, the one you perhaps suppose they have. Within themselves means *within the intimacy of that silent, multiple, diffuse touch.* And if you ask them insistently what they are thinking about, they can only reply: Nothing. Everything.

Thus what they desire is precisely nothing, and at the same time everything. Always something more and something else besides that *one*—sexual organ, for example—that you give them, attribute to them. Their desire is often interpreted and feared, as a sort of insatiable hunger, a voracity that will swallow you whole. Whereas it really involves a different economy more than anything else, one that upsets the linearity of a project, undermines the goal-object of a desire, diffuses the polarization toward a single pleasure, disconcerts fidelity to a single discourse.[28]

Recent interpretations have made it easy to use the life and work of Nietzsche to comprehend Irigaray's movement toward a politics that, because it demands unlimited receptivity, repudiates every finalizing synthesis, epistemology, ontology, or metaphysics. Nietzsche's determination to remain in ambiguities by politicizing all alleged facts was understandably hard to assimilate. Until recently, he has been interpreted so literally as to make him a proto-Nazi, an antifeminist, an advocate of nihilism. It has slowly become possible, however, to view him above all as treating

---

[28] Luce Irigaray, *This Sex Which Is Not One*, trans. Catherine Porter (Ithaca, N.Y.: Cornell University Press, 1985), pp. 28–30.

himself and the world as pervasively enacted—as *played.*[29] For him nothing was to be exempt: whatever appears to *be* is open to reconstruction. Challenging all reifications, Nietzsche provided a clearing in which every so-called entity, every thing, is but "the sum of its effects"—effects which are made to constitute entities such as male and female, master and slave, subject and object. What something *is,* whether it be sex or madness, depends altogether on the concerns of interpreters who *make* things cohere, who create connections, discourses, and compositions, who construct genealogies by composing one or another narrative. And what they include in the webs they spin depends precisely on *their* creative and re-creative power. Having power, they make things up, conceptualize, categorize. They invent traditions, transform conventions, change paradigms. They follow Nietzsche (or radical feminists) not by becoming Nietzscheans (or Radical Feminists) but by treating everything, especially themselves, as idiosyncratic and contingent, as free from unconditional, transhistorical meaning or truth, free from whatever might tie them to some universal nature or autonomous necessity. Engaged in politicking, playing, and performing, their works, like Nietzsche's *Thus Spoke Zarathustra,* are enactments—actualizations of the interminable process of politics. Their politics is not something that takes place outside their projects: it simply is their project.

Politics, in short, is not the end to which Nietzsche's work is the means. It is no more an ideal state which might be brought about by using his work as blueprint for an ideal society than Plato's *Republic.* Like play or dance or music—like Plato's interminable dialogues—politics is not good for anything beyond it. It's simply not useful, and therefore intolerable within a utilitarian, instrumentalist society. Sheer play, such politics is but the exhilarating exercise of enhancing knowledge, a joyous way of doing epistemology, a gay science, in Nietzsche's phrase. Such politics, such poetics, gives alien interests shelter within its infinitely contradictory structures.

To be sure, the presumptuousness of Nietzsche's hyperboles is hard to take. As his words turn into the flow of music, dance, and visual images,

---

[29] See Alexander Nehamas, *Nietzsche: Life as Literature* (Cambridge: Harvard University Press, 1985).

the culmination he keeps promising fails to be provided. Hearing Nietzsche, you await his message. He seems to be of several minds. You want to know what he really stands for, what his point is, what he really means you to do. Yet we are led on by the flow and overflow of his pronouncements, by his ensnaring confidence game. We remain in a state of suspense even as we recognize that his devices for holding us are political tricks: enigmatic declarations and contradictory voices, equivocations and parables, exaggerations and stories, but above all, captivating sentences (like and unlike those we serve in prison) which end with question marks and thus intimate the possibility of stays of execution, appeals, and reversals of judgment.

As my terms suggest, Nietzsche's performance, his very life, constitutes a practical demonstration of an all-comprehensive politics. Determined to acknowledge and save everything—to lose no votes—his politics clears space for integrating the most private and guarded of interests. It incorporates the welter of interests beyond the scope of conventional performances. Perverse, vulgar, brutal, nihilist, infantile, feminine interests—whatever is repressed and disparaged—is brought into play. Only the play itself—the dance of Nietzsche's words—is of ultimate import. The most radical of integrationists, he hyphenates purposefulness and purposelessness, destruction and construction, attack and retreat. He mobilizes metaphors, aphorisms, contradictions, and paradoxes to relate opposites. He celebrates nothing but the journey between open-ended symbols, nothing but an awesome emptiness in which to communicate with Otherness, the inarticulate, terrifying forces within oneself and one's environment.

Recognizing as much, his audiences can but interpret Nietzsche as it suits *them*. At best, they too will be endlessly dissembling and digressing, taking the most elaborate of detours, diverting themselves, becoming actors who take care of themselves by taking care of one another.

IF WE BELIEVE that coming to the point is of ultimate import, we are unable to take the full measure of Nietzsche's desperate poetics—his controlled trembling at the end, his minimal notebook entries before he ceased performing. We can scarcely esteem his politics as long as we believe in the possibility of escaping the drift toward the annihilation of human consciousness—and yet we also know that no other politics remains defensible. Swept along by currents not of our making, we realize that we can maintain our balance only by embracing a logic which legitimates active passivity, purposeful purposelessness, resolute irresolution, serious playfulness, hopeful hopelessness. The integration of such contradictions is so hard to handle that we understandably are more likely to think of someone as having integrity when he or she is loyal to a single ideal than when he playfully integrates a variety of ideals. We see him as speaking tongue-in-cheek. Not sharing his view that all that matters is how fully we can act here and now, we commit ourselves to less relativistic, more exclusive ideals. Denying that that progress is an illusion, that we are beyond recovery, we hold that a new consciousness will surely grow out of the purges and trials of modernity.

Even those who allow their works to prophesy the end of history retreat from their prophecies. Thus while Jean-Francois Lyotard maintained that contemporary society is inexorably universalizing instrumentalism because it judges all practices by the single criterion of efficiency and production he also found promise in postmodernism's rejection of global theories and transcultural foundations, its ourpouring of endless localized, context-bound projects.[30] Whereas Theodor Adorno foresaw humanity's being extinguished by its own instrumental reason which would extinguish all diversity, he also claimed that instrumental reason contains the seeds of its reversal.[31] Such hedging is reflected in William James's noting how strange it would be *not* to postulate something of

---

[30] See Jean-Francois Lyotard, *The Postmodern Condition* (Minneapolis: University of Minnesota Press, 1984) and "The Differend," *Diacritics* 14 (Fall 1984): 4–14. In an unpublished paper, Nancy Fraser and Linda Nicolson draw on Lyotard to reject transhistorical feminist critiques in favor of context-sensitive local ones. Yet like him they do not see postmodern practices as a noninstrumental, desperate strategy for maintaining a measure of independence from a state moving toward homogenizing society. Thus they hope that the course of instrumentalism can be reversed by a new avant-guarde armed with a "robust, postmodern-feminist paradigm." ("Social Criticism without Philosophy: An Encounter between Feminism and Postmodernism," paper presented at the meeting of the American Political Science Association, September 1987.)

[31] See Richard J. Bernstein, "The Rage against Reason," in Ernan McMullin, ed., *Construction and Constraint* (Notre Dame: University of Notre Dame Press, 1987), p. 197.

substance beyond mere survival: "The entire modern deification of survival *per se,* survival returning to itself, survival naked and abstract, with the denial of any substantive excellence in *what* survives, except for more survival still, is surely the strangest intellectual stopping-place ever proposed by one man to another." Failing to stop in that "strange" place, was James not encouraging himself to move toward identifying some "substantive excellence"?[32] And to what shelter is Jacques Derrida referring when he alludes to human "internality" as a basis for deconstructing an idealized humanism? And how could Einstein justify contradicting the logic of his physics by remarking that the universe was orderly, that God does not play dice and surely means well?[33] Is it not, finally, inhuman to reject that consoling impulse which logic and reason deny—that ambiguous ray of light Franz Kafka provided in the final chapter of *The Trial?* Though Kafka gave Joseph K. no chance to enact his death—to enact what remained of his life—he did allow him to look up as he was led to his execution. He looks up to "the top storey of the house adjoining the quarry. With a flicker as of a light going up, the casements of a window there suddenly flew open; a human figure, faint and insubstantial at that distance and that height, leaned abruptly forward and stretched both arms still farther. Who was it? A friend? A good man? Someone who wanted to help?"[34] Samuel Beckett's nonhero of *The Unnamable* ends his monologue within a blackness he knows to be impenetrable—and yet leaves a famous crack—a mere comma—between negation and affirmation, between present and future: "I can't go on, I'll go on."[35]

Can we manage without believing the impenetrable to be penetrable? Can we comprehend catastrophes without reducing them to music, rhyme, or narrative? Terror-struck, we are comforted by punctuation marks, by our languages, myths, rituals. Contributing to them, we construct edifices that console and sustain us. Thus the developmental stages

---

[32] Fred R. Dallmayr has called attention to Derrida's similar problematic in *Twilight of Subjectivity: Contributions to a Post-Individualist Theory of Politics* (Amherst: University of Massachusetts Press, 1981), p. 30.

[33] See Arthur Fine, "Einstein's Realism," in J. T. Cushing et al., *Science and Reality* (Notre Dame: University of Notre Dame Press, 1984).

[34] Franz Kafka, *The Trial* (New York: Knopf, 1937), p. 288.

[35] Samuel Beckett, *The Unnamable* (New York: Grove Press, 1958), p. 179.

designed by Freud, the dialectic movement of history designed by Marx, or the cadenced descent of man designed by Darwin impose language on what is otherwise brute power. In a postmythological era, we still work on myths that give us pause. Pauses, it turns out, are our last resort.

To encompass the enormities of the present, we follow paleolithic cave dwellers who came to *know* the animals which terrified them by depicting them. Despite the paralyzing silence of Hiroshima and Auschwitz we enlarge our consciousness by clearing space for play. We do what we can where we happen to be, act as Robert Altman did by creating a mythical *Nashville* where he orchestrated the contributions of a most mixed company of actors. Invited by Altman, they flew in from the corners of the world to perform, leaving it to him to reconcile and unify, to bring things to conclusions. And yet Altman declined to finish. The upbeat song that opens the film is repeated word for word at the end by a woman who faces a hysterical audience near panic. Everyone has moved through agony and death (one death in plain view) and the song's blue echoes now hold the weight of their experience:

> The price of bread may worry some
> But it don't worry me. . . .
> You may say, that I ain't free
> But it don't worry me. . . .
> And life may be a one-way street. . . .
> But it don't worry me. . . .

The music (it calms the audience following the assassination of one of the performers during her act) is contradicted not only by the slowly emerging smiles of children in the audience but by the film's own energetic persistence, by everyone's powerless-powerful, unworried-worried, unconcerned-concerned enactment of life's one-way street.

Coppola's *Apocalypse Now* shows Colonel Kurtz, a maverick officer, to be wholly composed after having outdistanced the all-controlling, all-absorbing logic of the machinery of war. He had experienced incomprehensible horror and worked to redeem it by ritualistically enacting it in off-limits territory under his own control. Coppola, however, leaves him no escape; in the precise language of the times, he is terminated. Nor does he allow Kurtz's unblinking assassin to return enlightened to the tidy structure of military command. He ends where he began, none the wiser. The Doors's music closes the film decisively: "This is the end. . . . " And yet the music which Copolla quotes and the fire which he displays deny his despair. However much the world is engulfed in flames, *he* is still quoting and displaying, still orchestrating and earning credit for making more movies. Beyond hope, he finds himself—we find ourselves—at last in that unbounded space which Eileen Simpson imagined for John Berryman (whose wife she was for eleven years), Robert Lowell, Ezra Pound, T. S. Eliot, and Delmore Schwartz. Reassembled in heaven, as she hoped, "they would recite one another's poems and talk for hours on end, free at last of worldly concerns about where the next advance, the next drink, the next girl or even the next inspiration would come from—free at last to be obsessed by poetry."[36] They would meet in that heaven where Jefferson had hoped Congress might be reassembled. There they would be at home with all the antinomies of existence, with every thesis and antithesis, at once in and out of this world.

FORTY YEARS AFTER Paul Tibbets piloted the B-29 that dropped the atomic bomb on Hiroshima, he sat down to lunch with David Remnick of the *Washington Post*.[37] Tibbets ordered quiche. As they ate and talked in a relaxed setting he remembered that just after the Japanese surrender he traveled to Nagasaki to observe the devastation there. He bought some handcarved trays, he told Remnick, and a few handmade rice bowls.

"The trays split," he said, "but the ricebowls, I still have those."

---

[36] Eileen Simpson, *Poets in Their Youth: A Memoir* (New York: Random House, 1982).

[37] Reported in the *Honolulu Star-Bulletin and Advertiser*, August 4, 1985, pp. A-1, A-4.

POSTSCRIPT

THERE is as yet no end to conferences, articles, and books on postmodernism. Still, in Venice and Paris intellectuals who are bonded in mutual antagonisms are dismissively shrugging their shoulders.

Don't you think, I remember one of them asking, that Umberto Eco's *Il nome della rosa* was easily reduced to a linear narrative by that 1986 movie? And hasn't Jacques Derrida really fallen back on an objectionable logocentrism in his very effort to deconstruct it?

Someone else asks if Richard Rorty's fashionable New Pragmatism doesn't ignore the suffocating, imperialist context necessary to decontextualize his praxis. Don't privileged American institutions like the University of Virginia ground his antifoundationalism?

And isn't Paul de Man's opportunistic anti-Semitic World War II journalism and his forgetting it protected by the rhetorical strategies of postmodernism?

It's certainly evident, isn't it, that legions of tenured semiotici have survived nothing more strenuous than the potlucks and the politics of academia. None of *their* tents ever went up in flames.

It's not surprising that those scholarly articles on intertextuality have finally reached such a degree of careerist rigor and tedious normalcy and ostentatious gravity that they just beg for new formulations.

What uncopyrighted language, they all seem to ask, can give voice to the inarticulate parts of the present?

Without responding to the boredom and uneasiness that provoke these questions, I have been framing a shelter for those engaged in an unacknowledged politics—*the politics of those who are determined to live lucidly while oppressed by the knowledge of the irresistible tendency of modernity to reduce all differences to sameness*. It is the politics of those in our midst who know this future to be implicitly present here and now.

The general resistance to their posture has made it easy for me to project (and now to recapitulate) the thrust as well as the context of their politics. For postmodernists, in my projection, contemporary systems ranging from welfare to warfare are mere functions of technological forces leading inexorably to the termination of the human venture. The countless successors of Shelley's *Frankenstein* and Goethe's *Faust* who have dramatized the deadly ramifications "progress" defined as a movement toward an autonomous technology have become mere entertainments within the culture of modernity. Countercultural enterprises are at most marginal efforts to decenter the impersonal forces of the world's military-industrial complexes. Ultimately nothing can deflect the nihilistic instrumentalism which, systemtically promoting the expansion of its own power, seduces and extinguishes whatever remains external to it. There is no way out, no new frontier, no virgin territory.

In this historical process, postmodernists seek to maintain consciousness. Distancing themselves from the movement toward extinction of consciousness while perceiving no escape from it, they maneuver not only to stay alive but to *enact* their lives. They maintain an awareness of mankind's prospects by desperately shuttling between an unmediated reality—the life-threatening artifacts of modernity—and a no less unmediated openness. Between these terminal points, they seek to keep their balance.

The sensibility of postmodernism is manifest not only in the arts but wherever men and women remain in action even while wholly aware of the bottomless contingency of every act, every happening, every word. Having come to terms with calamities, confinements, or tedium, such survivors are artists seeking to outperform the whirl of modernity, actors on improvised stages, espionage agents mapping treacherous terrain, children playfully testing the boundaries of reality. They are deft and shifty nomads careening through death-dealing territory. Painfully alert, ever apprehensive, they temporize in the face of obstinate realities. In transactions that are pervasively pragmatic they oblige themselves to keep deciding which rules, commitments, and identities are appropriate for the moment—that is, neither too light nor too heavy for going on. Thus they give expression to a social process of testing, negotiating, politicking.

Within this form of politics, postmodernists design and frame structures that make the most of the present. What they in fact succeed in making present—the reality they create—consists of whatever unperceived and unrealized elements they somehow manage to integrate in their structures. Magnifying and extending the present, they hold their own by speeding ahead of the torrents of modernization. Near despair, they provide temporary shelters for the speechless and the homeless, for whatever remains unspoken and alien in the imperium of modernity.

DEEPLY IMPLICATED IN the prevailing culture, too fatigued or embarrassed or resentful to embellish it, we speak of postmodernists as I have—in the third person plural. We say *they* are responding to the institutionalized terrors of our times by complacently affirming the worst and the best, the vulgar and the sublime, the fictitious and the real. It is *they* who fail to discriminate. It is *their* paranoia, *their* duplicity, *their* faithlessness, *their* recklessness. However mixed our feelings, *we* go on being trustworthy, loyal, truthful.

Too preoccupied to explore our own misgivings, we fail to come to terms with our deepest political impulse—the impulse which postmodernists express by living in contradiction, by relinquishing the comfort and ardor of ideology, by rejecting the worldview that divides society into an *us* and a *them*. We take sides and consecrate the purity of our perfectionism and our technology for enforcing it. Thus we insure ourselves so fully against Otherness that we deplete what resources remain for play and politics.

INDEX